Shine His Light 2: Directions In Life
Marie McGaha

Copyright ©Marie McGaha 2020
ISBN-13: 9781734284195

DWB PUBLISHING
www.dwbpublishing.com

Marie McGaha

For my mom, Blanch. I love you, Ma.

Introduction

This collection of devotionals are ones written depending on how I felt on any given day, or about what was going on in the world around me. Like anyone else, I have worries and fears. I don't like what's going on in the world, and especially in the United States, but I know that God is in control and everything will work out according to His plan.

The Bible tells us there will be turmoil and strife, and while I don't claim to always understand why life is the way it is, I do believe that God knows what He's doing. I believe that my life is in His hands, and that through my faith in Jesus Christ, no matter how crazy the world gets, He is going to take care of me.

No matter what is going on in your life, or what your fears may be right now, God has an answer for you. He has a plan for your life. Be of good courage for the Lord goes before you in all that you do (Deuteronomy 31:6).

Cast Your Cares

"Do not be anxious or worried about anything, but in everything [every circumstance and situation] by prayer and petition with thanksgiving, continue to make your [specific] requests known to God. And the peace of God [that peace which reassures the heart, that peace] which transcends all understanding, [that peace which] stands guard over your hearts and your minds in Christ Jesus [is yours]."
~Philippians 4:6-7 (Amplified Bible)

I don't use the Amplified Bible often, but I like the way it expands on this verse. I see so many people worrying, stressed out and anxious about everything in their lives. They are living in the exact opposite way the Bible tells us to. I used to worry over bills, jobs, my kids, and everything else in life but my worrying never changed anything. It did make me tense, angry, stressed out, depressed, and fearful, which is not how the Lord tells us to live.

"And which of you by being anxious can add a single hour to his span of life? If then you are not able to do as small a thing as that, why are you anxious about the rest? (Luke 12:25-26)."

Worry never has a positive impact on our lives; it does, however, have some negative consequences. According to Web MD, "Chronic worrying can affect your daily life so much that it may interfere with your appetite, lifestyle habits, relationships, sleep and job performance. Many people who worry excessively are so anxiety-ridden that they seek relief in harmful lifestyle habits such as overeating, cigarette smoking, or using alcohol and drugs." It can also lead to physical ailments such as headaches, stomach up-set, high blood pressure, and chest pains.

Worry is like sitting in a rocking chair - it gives you something to do but it doesn't accomplish much.

"Cast your burden on the Lord, and He will sustain you; He will never permit the righteous to be moved (Psalm 55:22)."

"Humble yourselves, therefore, under the mighty hand of God so that at the proper time He may exalt you, casting all your anxieties on Him, because He cares for you (1 Peter 5:6-7)."

It's Not About the Money

"Someone in the crowd said to Him, "Teacher, tell my brother to divide the inheritance with me." But He said to him, "Man, who made Me a judge or arbitrator over you?" And He said to them, "Take care, and be on your guard against all covetousness, for one's life does not consist in the abundance of his possessions."
~Luke 12:13-15

Like most working-class Americans, we live paycheck to paycheck. The bills are paid, we don't want for anything but there's not much left over either. That is sometimes very frustrating considering the hours and effort put into earning those paychecks. It seems every time we might get a little bit ahead, something comes up and there goes the extra. On top of that, prices edge upward every day. The last time I filled up my truck's tank, gas was nineteen cents a gallon higher than the month before! But I remember when I was a kid and my parents complaining about the same things - not enough money and rising prices. However, the Bible tells us not to worry about those things because God takes care of His people.

"So, do not worry, saying, 'What shall we eat?' or 'What shall we drink?' or 'What shall we wear?' For the pagans run after all these things, and your heavenly Father knows that you need them. But seek first His kingdom and His righteousness, and all these things will be given to you as well (Matthew 6:31-33)."

We live in a world that worships excess and no matter how much people have, it's never enough. We see teens dealing drugs because wearing gold chains and driving big cars and living the "thug life" is better than getting an education and earning a living.

We see the rise and demise of Hollywood stars as they strive to be rich and famous. Television shows offer recording contracts to hopeful contestants who want to be the next big singing star. But how many 'one hit wonders' have we seen over the years who are here today and gone tomorrow?

"Not that I am speaking of being in need, for I have learned in whatever situation I am to be content. I know how to be brought low, and I know how to abound. In any and every circumstance, I have learned the secret of facing plenty and hunger, abundance and need. I can do all things through Him who strengthens me (Philippians 4:11-13.)"

We all go through highs and lows in life and knowing that God is in control of every situation is how we get through each day. It isn't how much we earn, how big our bank accounts are, or the kind of car we drive that impresses God. It's our love for Him, for others, and the condition and motives of our hearts that matter.

We work to pay our bills and there's nothing wrong with living paycheck to paycheck. If we inherit a million bucks, there's nothing wrong with that either. It's how we live with what we have that matters. Go to church, study God's word, pay your tithes, serve God by serving others. Those things matter to God, and what matters to God is what should matter to us.

"The one who offers thanksgiving as his sacrifice glorifies Me; to the one who orders his way rightly I will show the salvation of God (Psalm 50:23)!"

The Battle is Real

"The night is far gone; the day is at hand. So then let us cast off the works of darkness and put on the armor of light."
~Romans 13:12

This is one of my favorite verses, although, I must admit, when I first read it in my youth, I had no idea what it meant. But being me, sort of like a dog with a bone, I don't let go of anything until I understand the spiritual, physical and meta-physical meanings. I chewed on that verse for years! It may seem that elementary, it means to stop living in sin (darkness) and to live in the light (salvation). But I think it has a much deeper, richer meaning for us.

In Jesus' day, and prior to His life on Earth, battles against invading armies were common. When warriors rested at night they wore a different type of armor that was heavy and cumbersome. It served two purposes - to protect them from the elements, and to protect them from a sneak attack while they slept. When dawn approached, the took off the heavier armor for a lighter type that allowed more freedom of movement to engage their enemy in battle.

In Romans 13:12, Paul uses this metaphor of taking off one thing and trading it for another. Certainly, when we experience salvation in Jesus Christ, we come out of the darkness of sin into the light of forgiveness and redemption. As we grow in Christ, we also take off the ignorance of not understanding our place in the Kingdom and put on the full maturity of Christ's nature.

"Again, Jesus spoke to them, saying, 'I am the light of the world. Whoever follows Me will not walk in darkness but will have the light of life' (John 8:12)."

When we contrast Romans with the above verse, we see that it is only by Jesus that we come out of the darkness that engulfs our souls. But it's there that the real battle begins. We are now on satan's hit list. The battle is real, and we must fight like soldiers, fully covered in armor.

"Finally, be strong in the Lord and in the strength of His might. Put on the whole armor of God, that you may be able to stand against the schemes of the devil. For we do not wrestle against flesh and blood, but against the rulers, against the authorities, against the cosmic powers over this present darkness, against the spiritual forces of evil in the heavenly places. Therefore, take up the whole armor of God, that you may be able to withstand in the evil day, and having done all, to stand firm (Ephesians 6:10-13)."

When we look at the Old Testament, we see the physical battles the Children of Israel went through to possess the land promised to Abraham. Even then, the battle belonged to the Lord (2 Chronicles 20:15). In every physical battle, there was a spiritual battle. When God's people did as the Lord said, the battle was won. When they ignored the Lord's commands, their enemies won. The battle remains the same for us. When we listen to the Lord and obey Him, victory is ours every time.

"But you are a chosen race, a royal priest-hood, a holy nation, a people for His own possession, that you may proclaim the excellencies of Him who called you out of darkness into His marvelous light (1 Peter 2:9)."

The Death of the Saints

"I bless the Lord who gives me counsel; in the night also my heart instructs me. I have set the Lord always before me; because He is at my right hand, I shall not be shaken."
~Psalm16:7-8

My father went home to be with the Lord July 16, 2019. As sorry as I feel for myself, my siblings and our mother, my heart rejoices because my Pop is in Heaven where I want to be. I can't imagine what it's like to finally stand before our Lord and Savior. My Pop was 82 and served the Lord for many years. He has earned his rest.

Many people, even some Christians, think of Heaven as an abstract place. And I know some Christians who still fear death. Personally, I look forward to the day I leave this planet and join my family members who have gone before me, but most of all, I want to see Jesus face to face. After all, isn't that our ultimate destination?

"So, we are always of good courage. We know that while we are at home in the body we are away from the Lord, for we walk by faith, not by sight. Yes, we are of good courage, and we would rather be away from the body and at home with the Lord (2 Corinthians 5:6-8)."

There's a saying I like: Earth is not my home; I'm just passing through on my way to Heaven. That is true for every blood-bought Christian alive today. For everyone who has accepted Christ as their Savior, has confessed with their mouth that Jesus is Lord, and has called upon His name, the reward is

everlasting life with Him in a brand-new body free of
pain and sorrow.

*"He will wipe away every tear from their eyes,
and death shall be no more, neither shall there be
mourning, nor crying, nor pain anymore, for the for-
mer things have passed away (Revelation 21:4)."*

We live in mortal bodies with aches and pains.
The evidence of our mortality grows ever clearer with
each passing year. Life without pain, sorrow, suffering, anger, war, and all the other things we live with
every day may seem like a dream, but in Christ, that
is our reality when we close our eyes to this life.
My father is free of the pain in his body brought on by
advancing age and the cancer he's fought so valiantly.
He is rejoicing with the saints of Heaven right now and
probably has hugged the stuffing out of Jesus. He is
where I want to be. Where each of us should want to
be.

*"Precious in the eyes of the Lord is the death of His
saints (Psalm 116:15)."*

The Last Word

"He who testifies to these things says, "Surely I am coming soon." Amen. Come, Lord Jesus!"
~Revelation 22:20

When I was younger, I thought this verse, and others about Jesus' return, wasn't all that important. After all, I'd heard all about the Rapture since I was a little kid, and my grandmother patiently awaited that moment when the Lord would show up amid thunder, a shout and the blast of the Shofar. She believed the Lord would return in her lifetime. As I got older and had more understanding of the hope my grandmother had in Christ's return, I also began to have that same hope. Even the disciples believed Christ's Second Coming would occur in their lifetime. I suppose every generation since then has believed they would see the coming of the Lord. I know I certainly do.

"Let not your hearts be troubled. Believe in God; believe also in me. In my Father's house are many rooms. If it were not so, would I have told you that I go to prepare a place for you. And if I go and prepare a place for you, I will come again and will take you to myself, that where I am you may be also. And you know the way to where I am going (John 14:1-4)."

We don't have to know when the Lord will take us home, whether at His Second Coming or through our bodily death. What we must know is that one way or the other, we will see Him again. We must be ready no matter when we are called home.

Jesus' last words, "I am coming soon," may occur in my lifetime, and what a wonderful event that will be to see first-hand. However, if He doesn't, is there any less hope in my heart? Of course not. My hope is not in an event, it is in the person of Jesus Christ, who gave His life that I would have mine. That is the hope of Glory. One day, I will leave this body and all its aches and pains, and step from this life into eternal life with my one true hope, the Lord Himself. The last words Jesus said in this life will be forgotten as soon as I hear the first words He speaks to me in His kingdom: *"Well done, good and faithful servant (Matthew 25:21)."*

"But at midnight there was a cry, 'Here is the bridegroom! Come out to meet him.' Then all those virgins rose and trimmed their lamps. And the foolish said to the wise, 'Give us some of your oil, for our lamps are going out.' But the wise answered, saying, 'Since there will not be enough for us and for you, go rather to the dealers and buy for yourselves.' And while they were going to buy, the bridegroom came, and those who were ready went in with him to the marriage feast, and the door was shut. Afterward the other virgins came also, saying, 'Lord, lord, open to us.' But he answered, 'Truly, I say to you, I do not know you.' Watch therefore, for you know neither the day nor the hour (Matthew 25:6-13)."

Wars & Rumors of Wars

"Immediately after the tribulation of those days the sun will be darkened, and the moon will not give its light, and the stars will fall from heaven, and the powers of the heavens will be shaken. Then will appear in Heaven the sign of the Son of Man, and then all the tribes of the Earth will mourn, and they will see the Son of Man coming on the clouds of Heaven with power and great glory. And He will send out His angels with a loud trumpet call, and they will gather His elect from the four winds, from one end of heaven to the other."
~Matthew 24:29-31

I have always been fascinated with the end of life as we know it here on planet Earth. The wars, rumors of wars, and all the other things that must take place before Jesus Christ returns. I was raised to believe in the pre-tribulation Rapture theory that all Christians will be called off the Earth before any of the really bad stuff happens. In 1995, the Lord began to show me things that changed my mind. I no longer believe that Christians are exempt from what is coming in the last days. If you believe in a pre-tribulation rapture, I'm not here to change your mind. If I'm correct, you'll know soon enough, and if you're correct, it's not going to matter to either of us.

The reason I'm writing this is because our lives may change very soon in ways we could never imagine. No matter what we believe about our futures, we must be more concerned with our eternal future. Whether a pre-tribulation rapture, a mid-tribulation rapture, or a post-tribulation rapture, our eternal destination is being determined right now.

"For He says, "In a favorable time I listened to you, and in a day of salvation I have helped you." Behold, now is the favorable time; behold, now is the day of salvation (2 Corinthians 6:2)."

No matter where you are or what you've done, the heart of God is calling out to you. We don't know what tomorrow will bring or if we'll be here to see it. However, we do know none of us are getting out of here alive, and the choice we make right now will determine our eternal future. Jesus is calling out to you, don't ignore Him.

"Therefore do not be ashamed of the testimony about our Lord, nor of me His prisoner, but share in suffering for the gospel by the power of God, who saved us and called us to a holy calling, not because of our works but because of His own purpose and grace, which He gave us in Christ Jesus before the ages began, and which now has been manifested through the appearing of our Savior Christ Jesus, who abolished death and brought life and immortality to light through the gospel (2 Timothy 1:8-10)."

Grieving God's Heart

"If you are insulted for the name of Christ, you are blessed, because the Spirit of glory and of God rests upon you."
~1 Peter 4:14

I've seen a lot in life. I've seen things I wish I hadn't. I've seen things I hope no one else ever does. There's not much in this world that surprises or shocks me, except people. And not just the average non-Christian running amok, but people who profess to be Christians and love God. Yet their actions and the words of their mouths show the opposite.

"But no human being can tame the tongue. It is a restless evil, full of deadly poison. With it we bless our Lord and Father, and with it we curse people who are made in the likeness of God. From the same mouth come blessing and cursing. My brothers, these things ought not to be so (James 3:8-10)."

For Christians, our lives are to be modeled after Christ. To walk in love, to be at peace with others, and to show others through our words and deeds that we follow Jesus. Our goal is to bring the light of Jesus into the lives of a desperate and decaying world. So, what do we accomplish by attacking other believers? Is that showing Christ in you? Is that appealing to anyone who doesn't know Christ? And what does it say about you if all you can do is criticize and condemn?

"Let no corrupting talk come out of your mouths, but only such as is good for building up, as fits the

occasion, that it may give grace to those who hear (Ephesians 4:29)."

There is so much trash in the world, and as Christians, we must be above it. We serve one God in Jesus Christ. We are saved by the same Spirit, and it is the same blood at Calvary that Jesus shed for us all. When I hear Christians bad-mouth other Christians, it makes me sad because it grieves the very heart of God. This should not be so among believers in Christ.

"See that no one repays anyone evil for evil, but always seek to do good to one another and to everyone (1 Thessalonians 5:15)."

Your Choice

*"I perceived that whatever God does endures for-
ever; nothing can be added to it, nor anything taken
from it. God has done it, so that people fear before
Him. That which is, already has been; that which is
to be, already has been; and God seeks what has
been driven away."*
~Ecclesiastes 3:14-15

     "What's gonna happen already has. The only
thing you can do is your very best, and remember,
you only get one chance to make a good first impres-
sion." That's the advice I've given my kids on nume-
rous occasions. The last time was just a couple of
weeks ago when my youngest son called while on his
way to the "most important interview" of his life.
     Our lives have a determined pattern; we are
born, go through stages of growth, go to school,
graduate, get a job, meet the right person, get married, have kids and the process starts all over again.
Hopefully, along the way we have good people in our
lives who show us by example how to make the most
out of life, but all too often that isn't the case.
     We don't always get the great parents. We
don't always get born into the best family. We don't
get the greatest opportunities in education or jobs.
We don't always meet the right person. Sometimes
it seems like everything that can go wrong does. But
no matter what, we always have the opportunity to
make better choices.

*"When a man's ways please the Lord, He makes even
his enemies to be at peace with him. Better is a little with righteousness than great revenues with*

injustice. *The heart of man plans his way, but the Lord establishes his steps (Proverbs 16:7-9)."*

No matter what left turns we have taken, or how messed up our lives become, we can make the choice to find a better direction. The way of right-eousness may seem far off, but God is as close as a single prayer and He will change your life if you allow Him to.

"There is therefore now no condemnation for those who are in Christ Jesus. For the law of the Spirit of life has set you free in Christ Jesus from the law of sin and death. For God has done what the law, weakened by the flesh, could not do. By sending His own Son in the likeness of sinful flesh and for sin, He condemned sin in the flesh, in order that the righteous requirement of the law might be fulfilled in us, who walk not according to the flesh but according to the Spirit (Romans 8:1-4)."

No matter where we are, where we've been, or what we've done, as long as there is breath in our body, we have the opportunity to change where we're going. We have choices in life, and no matter what those around us are saying or doing, we can choose to change the road we're on. We choose what to say, how to respond in any given situation, and when we make a choice, we are also choosing the consequences of life or death. When we choose to continue down the path that has already shown us nothing good, we are choosing death. When we make the choice for change, and follow the path God wants us on, we choose life.

"Now therefore fear the Lord and serve Him in

sincerity and in faithfulness. Put away the gods that your fathers served beyond the River and in Egypt and serve the Lord. And if it is evil in your eyes to serve the Lord, choose this day whom you will serve, whether the gods your fathers served in the region beyond the River, or the gods of the Amorites in whose land you dwell. But as for me and my house, we will serve the Lord (Joshua 24:14-15)."

Remember the last line of Ecclesiastes 3:15 above... *"God seeks what has been driven away."* If you're lost, you can be found. God will always answer those who seek Him with a right heart, and He will answer those who ask with right motives.

My son got the job he interviewed for.

What God Knows

"And He made from one man every nation of man-kind to live on all the face of the Earth, having de-termined allotted periods and the boundaries of their dwelling place, that they should seek God, and perhaps feel their way toward Him and find Him. Yet He is actually not far from each one of us, for 'In Him we live and move and have our be-ing'; as even some of your own poets have said, 'For we are in-deed His offspring.' Being then God's off-spring, we ought not to think that the divine being is like gold or silver or stone, an image formed by the art and imagination of man. The times of igno-rance God overlooked, but now He commands all people every-where to repent, because He has fixed a day on which He will judge the world in righteousness by a man whom He has appointed; and of this He has given assurance to all by raising Him from the dead."
~Acts 17:26-31

I love the book of Acts and especially chapter seventeen. Having begun in Thessalonica, where the gospel was not well-received, Paul had been sent to Berea, and then taken to Greece, where he preach-ed salvation through Jesus Christ, while all around him was man-made idols and people spouting off the latest in beliefs. Paul observed that the people were religious, and even had an idol dedicated to "the un-known god." These people, unlike those in Thessalo-nica and Berea, were seeking someone, something, some god to worship. Not knowing who the true God was, they worshipped whatever idol someone else said was the one to worship. They were far off the mark trying to fill the God-shaped hole within them, but they were looking for something real to believe in.

Looking around the world today, I see the same thing. People are still trying to fill the God-shaped hole within them, yet they are doing it with false gods instead of the only true God, Jesus Christ. We see people following after musicians, movie and television stars, athletes, philosophers, authors, and other people who have no better answer than the person next to them. We see people lusting after fame and fortune with the belief those things will make them happy and fulfilled. Yet, for all the glamor in the world, for all the riches, bright lights, and glory from adoring fans, we see more depression and unhappiness than ever before. We will never feel content, complete, or fulfilled by the things of this world because those things are temporary and only make us happy for a moment. When the moment is gone, we move on to the next thing that will cure our ills.

"Do not lay up for yourselves treasures on Earth, where moth and rust destroy and where thieves break in and steal, but lay up for yourselves treasures in heaven, where neither moth nor rust destroys and where thieves do not break in and steal. For where your treasure is, there your heart will be also (Matthew 6:19-21)."

"But godliness with contentment is great gain, for we brought nothing into the world, and we cannot take anything out of the world. But if we have food and clothing, with these we will be content. But those who desire to be rich fall into temptation, into a snare, into many senseless and harmful

desires that plunge people into ruin and destruction (1 Timothy 6:6-9)."

I am not encouraged when I look at the world. In fact, I am pretty much disgusted by what I see. The lack of morals, respect, values, and work ethic on every level of society is abhorrent. And through my eyes, I see no hope, no future, or any way possible for things to change. However, my eyes do not see what God sees. My eyes cannot tell one thing from another, they cannot see the future, and certainly, I cannot see into the hearts of other people. But God can. He knows the deepest, most inner secrets in each of us. He knows the beginning to the end, and there is nothing hidden from Him. He knows how all of this is going to work out and which of us is on the verge of making the decision to stop following false gods, to start worshipping the one true God, and that is what I must place my faith in. God is in control and He knows what He's doing.

"Where shall I go from Your Spirit? Or where shall I flee from Your presence? If I ascend to heaven, You are there! If I make my bed in Sheol, You are there! If I take the wings of the morning and dwell in the uttermost parts of the sea, even there Your hand shall lead me, and Your right hand shall hold me. If I say, 'Surely the darkness shall cover me, and the light about me be night," even the darkness is not dark to You; the night is bright as the day, for darkness is as light with You' (Psalm 139:7-12)."

One Thing I Ask

"One thing have I asked of the Lord, that will I seek after: that I may dwell in the house of the Lord all the days of my life, to gaze upon the beauty of the Lord and to inquire in His temple. For He will hide me in His shelter in the day of trouble; He will conceal me under the cover of His tent; He will lift me high upon a rock."
~Psalm 27:4-5

No matter what I do for the Lord in this life, it will never be enough to repay Him for what He has done for me. My life was a wreck. I was not just in need of salvation, I needed complete renovation. I was like a house that looked great from the outside but when you walked inside, you could see the deterioration and knew that house would have to be gutted and completely redone before it could be habitable. My inner self was the same way. Years of childhood sexual abuse through abuse as an adult, drugs, alcohol, depression, suicidal ideation, to name a few of my ongoing list of problems, made me inhabitable. My mind was a wreck, my emotions were out of control, and I didn't know whether I was coming or going, but whichever way it was, it was the wrong way.

I had no help, no hope, no future, no vision for a better life, and at that point, death would have been the perfect answer... or so I thought. What changed my life? I met someone who cared about me, who wanted better for me than I wanted for myself, and I latched on to him. No, it wasn't God, it was my late husband, Bear. The dynamics there would take way too long to explain but he was a life raft when I was sinking. What I didn't know, and what Bear didn't know, is that God was going to use that relationship for both of our benefits. And that's exactly what He did. That was more than 30 years ago and although Bear has gone home to the Lord, I have never forgotten where I came from or, more importantly, where I would have gone had God not intervened. I was on that wide road to hell, and so was Bear. God had answered the prayers of both our praying grandmothers even though both had gone home many years earlier.

"Enter by the narrow gate. For the gate is wide and the way is easy that leads to destruction, and those who enter by it are many. For the gate is narrow and the way is hard that leads to life, and those who find it are few (Matthew 7:13-14)."

In the years since marrying Bear, since coming back to the Lord where I belonged, I have done everything I can to make sure that others know there is a better way. I have done everything I know how to do to bring the message of hope in Christ to others, and to share my life of horrors to help others see that no matter how bad life is, Jesus is the only answer. No matter what kind of life you lead, one of hell on Earth or one of palatial luxury, Jesus is still the only answer.

One day this life will end and each of us will stand before God and answer for our lives. I always imagined God would ask, "Why did you do drugs? Why did you sin? Why were you such a horrible person?" But that isn't what God is going to ask. We will have to give account for our deeds and words, but I think God's only question is going to be, "Why didn't you accept Jesus Christ as your Savior when you had the chance?" I think God's heart is breaking over each one that has to hear that question.

Life isn't easy, it's hard for everyone. We make mistakes. Sometimes, we make huge mistakes that can't be righted by saying, "I'm sorry." Sometimes, we have to pay for our mistakes in ways we could never imagine. But no matter how big the mistakes, no matter how awful our lives may have been, or continue to be, no matter what happened to us as children that we had no control over, no matter where we came from, we can all make the determination of where we will go when this life ends.

Jesus is the answer. He can heal our wounds, our minds, our bodies, and make us whole again. But we must take the first step of accepting Him as our Lord and Savior. It doesn't mean our lives will start popping up all rosy and beautiful, but it does mean we will be on the road to healing. We may still have to answer for the deeds done prior to knowing Jesus because the laws of the universe don't change. When we choose an action, we also choose the consequences. Sometimes, society requires we pay those consequences in ways we'd rather not but regardless of how payment is garnered, Christ is still with us.

Don't wait until it's too late. Don't wait until you stand before God and have to answer, "Why didn't you accept my Son?" Allow Jesus into your heart and life so that the healing can begin now, and when you stand in eternity before God, you will hear, "Well done, My child. Welcome to Heaven!" No matter what sins you may have committed, none are too great for God to forgive.

"For the grace of God has appeared, bringing salvation for all people, training us to renounce

ungodliness and worldly passions, and to live self-control-led, upright, and godly lives in the present age, waiting for our blessed hope, the appearing of the glory of our great God and Savior Jesus Christ, who gave Himself for us to redeem us from all lawlessness (sins) and to purify for Himself a people for His own possession who are zealous for good works (Titus 2:11-14)."

If you haven't accepted Christ, do it now, it's not difficult. Say, "Jesus, I know I've sinned, and I need You to save me. I accept You as my Lord and Savior and ask You to live in my heart. Thank you Lord for dying for me so that I can live for You. In Jesus' Holy Name, Amen."

Yes, it's that simple. You are now a child of the Most High God if you said that prayer and meant it. So, what's next? Find a Bible believing church, go to several and see which one makes you feel at home. I prefer small, independent churches over the larger ones because I don't feel like I get lost in the crowd. Buy a Bible or download one on your phone. There are many versions. I prefer the New King James Version (NKJV), and the English Standard Version (ESV), but read a few different ones to see what is easiest for you. And go to church every time the doors open. Read your Bible every day. Pray. Pray. Pray. Every day. Listen to Christian music and worship the Lord every day. Your life is about to change in ways you never thought possible because now, you are a new creation! Hallelujah!

"Therefore, if anyone is in Christ, he is a new creation. The old has passed away; behold, the new has come. All this is from God, who through Christ reconciled us to Himself and gave us the ministry of

34

reconciliation; that is, in Christ God was reconciling the world to Himself, not counting their trespasses against them, and entrusting to us the message of reconciliation. Therefore, we are ambassadors for Christ, God making His appeal through us. We implore you on behalf of Christ, be reconciled to God. For our sake He made Him to be sin who knew no sin, so that in Him we might become the righteousness of God (2 Corinthians 5:17-21)."

The Seasons of Life

"For everything there is a season, and a time for every matter under heaven: a time to be born, and a time to die; a time to plant, and a time to pluck up what is planted; a time to kill, and a time to heal; a time to break down, and a time to build up; a time to weep, and a time to laugh; a time to mourn, and a time to dance; a time to cast away stones, and a time to gather stones together; a time to embrace, and a time to refrain from embracing; a time to seek, and a time to lose; a time to keep, and a time to cast away; a time to tear, and a time to sew; a time to keep silence, and a time to speak; a time to love, and a time to hate; a time for war, and a time for peace."
~Ecclesiastes 3:1-9

Everything in the world runs in cycles; that is how God created things, including us. We see the cycles in everyday life - clocks, calendars, work schedules, the weather, and our very lives. We are conceived in our mother's womb; we grow and develop at a certain rate and are born at a certain time. We grow as children, become adolescents, young adults, and the cycle begins again with us as we marry and have our own children. In the Disney movie, *The Lion King*, one of the songs is called "Circle of Life."

"It's the circle of life
And it moves us all
Through despair and hope
Through faith and love
Till we find our place
On the path unwinding

In the circle
The circle of life..."
(©1994 Elton John)

We all live in this circle of life and there's nothing we can do that stops it. It is what some call the "law of the universe," but in reality, it's the law of Almighty God. When God calls something into being, it cannot be undone. We are all the creation of His mighty hand. There is nothing created that was not created by Him, through Him, and because of Him (Colossians 1:16). All life was created by Him, and that includes the planet we live on. He created it in perfect proportion to suit the human body's need for different elements, food, oxygen, sun, rain, and wind. Everything serves a purpose under the hand of God. For humans, our purpose is to serve Him, worship Him, and then spend eternity with Him. When we stray from that purpose, we suffer consequences just like Adam and Eve did when they disobeyed God.

"And to Adam He said, 'Because you have listened to the voice of your wife and have eaten of the tree of which I commanded you, you shall not eat of it, cursed is the ground because of you; in pain you shall eat of it all the days of your life; thorns and thistles it shall bring forth for you; and you shall eat the plants of the field. By the sweat of your face you shall eat bread, till you return to the ground, for out of it you were taken; for you are dust, and to dust you shall return (Genesis 3:17-19)."

Humans have been disobeying God since the beginning and we continue to do so to this day. No matter what we are told, or what we experience, we continue to go back to our sins despite the pain it causes. As the saying goes, the definition of insanity is doing the same thing over and over and expecting a different outcome. Why do we do it? What is the appeal of a painful life? I have theories but as a human who was caught up in the cycle of insanity, expecting different outcomes even though I was doing the same things over and over, I can't explain why we do what we do. Some say it is human nature to do things the hard way, and while I suppose that's true to an extent, it's still not an explanation, it's just a rationale. So, what is our true purpose here on Earth, our purpose under the sun?

"Know that the Lord is God. It is He who made us, and we are His; we are His people, the sheep of His pasture (Psalm 100:3)."

There may be things that we cannot control – the sun is going to come up when it comes up; the wind is going to blow where it will; the rain is going to fall upon all the Earth; we are going to follow the cycle of life - birth, growth, marriage, death, just like those before us did; but we don't have to follow a path that leads us to hell. That much is within our control. We have free will, we can choose Who to follow. We can decide the path of our souls, and as long as there is breath in our bodies, we can choose to stop living like we can't wait to get to hell and start living like Heaven is waiting for us.

"The end of the matter; all has been heard. Fear God and keep his commandments, for this is the whole duty of man. For God will bring every deed

into judgment, with every secret thing, whether good or evil (Ecclesiastes 12:13-14)."

Grow Up

"Children, obey your parents in the Lord, for this is right. Honor your father and mother (this is the first commandment with a promise), that it may go well with you and that you may live long in the land."
~Ephesians 6:1-3

Every Mother's Day makes me a little sentimental as I think about how quickly the years flew by and my kids grew up. Even though it's the order of things, as parents, we don't realize how quickly time flies until our kids are out of the house and on their own. I miss the days when my kids were little. I miss the handprint drawings and papier mache flowers. I miss being the only woman in my sons' lives, and I miss being the only comfort for my daughters. I miss the sound of giggles and footsteps and fingerprints on the walls. I miss all of that, but I realize that I also seem to have forgotten all the fighting, screaming, yelling, arguing; beds that were never made, laundry never put away, garbage never taken out, and all the other things that also go with being a parent. We tend to romanticize the past once it's the past and not our everyday life. There's a lot to be said for growing up, too.

"When I was a child, I spoke like a child, I thought like a child, I reasoned like a child. When I became a man, I gave up childish ways (1 Corinthians 13:11)."

We are all expected to grow up. Even God expects us to grow up in Him. We don't expect our children to stay in the infancy stage, the toddler stage, or the teen stage. We want them to grow, learn and mature, and eventually, be on their own and start their own families. God wants the same type of growth in us.

When we come to Him, newly saved, unsure of our first steps in Christ, He gives us His Holy Spirit as a guide, and directs us to churches, to pastors, to teachers, and others who can help us grow in His word and His ways. It is our path in life to grow and spread the gospel to others, to lend a hand to help others grow in God, and to become mature Christian men and women.

Just as we expect our children to grow and leave behind their youthful pursuits and immaturity, God expects us to do the same (2 Timothy 2:22). Growing up isn't easy but that's why there are parents and grandparents to help us along the way. Once we are grown, however, we are expected to act accordingly. We are expected to earn our own living, pay bills, raise our own kids, and to act responsibly as mature adults. God expects nothing less.

"But solid food is for the mature, for those who have their powers of discernment trained by constant practice to distinguish good from evil (Hebrews 5:14)."

I miss the children my kids used to be, but I am madly in love with the men and women they've become. They are no longer children subject to the whims and careless pursuits of youth. They no longer base decisions on what their friends do, or what they think they can get away with if mom doesn't know about it. They have grown up and act accordingly. When we, as children of God, continue to act as though we have no direction, or pursue things contrary to God's word, then we are not growing in

Christ but are instead, hanging on to the things of the world; to the things of the past that made us feel good or gave us a sense of worth – even if that really wasn't the case. We must put away our childish whims and grow in the Lord, becoming like Christ and being set apart from the world.

"And He gave the apostles, the prophets, the evangelists, the shepherds and teachers, to equip the saints for the work of ministry, for building up the body of Christ, until we all attain to the unity of the faith and of the knowledge of the Son of God, to mature manhood, to the measure of the stature of the fullness of Christ, so that we may no longer be children, tossed to and fro by the waves and carried about by every wind of doctrine, by human cunning, by craftiness in deceitful schemes (Ephesians 4:11-14)."

Do The Math: 70x7=490

"Then Peter came to Him and said, 'Lord, how often shall my brother sin against me, and I forgive him? Up to seven times?' Jesus said to him, 'I do not say to you, up to seven times, but up to seventy times seven.'"
~Matthew 18:21-22

Some versions of the Bible translate the number of times as 77, but I like this version of 70 times 7, which comes to 490 times per day! In other words, no matter how many times someone does something to hurt us, we are to forgive them. Even though forgiveness can be difficult, it is possible to forgive even the most horrendous acts against us. Especially when we keep in mind all the things Christ forgave us for.

When we fail to forgive, we continue to carry the pain of the offense wherever we go. It colors everything we do, and often destroys new relationships before they even get started. Unforgiveness makes us bitter, resentful, and angry. And it keeps us focused on the past. You cannot move forward in Christ if your focus is behind you.

"Not that I have already obtained this or am already perfect, but I press on to make it my own, because Christ Jesus has made me His own. Brothers, I do not consider that I have made it my own. But one thing I do: forgetting what lies behind and straining forward to what lies ahead, I press on toward the goal for the prize of the upward call of God in Christ Jesus (Philippians 3:12-14)."

Marie McGaha

Do The Math: 70x7=490

"Then Peter came to Him and said, 'Lord, how often shall my brother sin against me, and I forgive him? Up to seven times?' Jesus said to him, 'I do not say to you, up to seven times, but up to seventy times seven.'"
~Matthew 18:21-22

Some versions of the Bible translate the number of times as 77, but I like this version of 70 times 7, which comes to 490 times per day! In other words, no matter how many times someone does something to hurt us, we are to forgive them. Even though forgiveness can be difficult, it is possible to forgive even the most horrendous acts against us. Especially when we keep in mind all the things Christ forgave us for.

When we fail to forgive, we continue to carry the pain of the offense wherever we go. It colors everything we do, and often destroys new relationships before they even get started. Unforgiveness makes us bitter, resentful, and angry. And it keeps us focused on the past. You cannot move forward in Christ if your focus is behind you.

"Not that I have already obtained this or am already perfect, but I press on to make it my own, because Christ Jesus has made me His own. Brothers, I do not consider that I have made it my own. But one thing I do: forgetting what lies behind and straining forward to what lies ahead, I press on toward the goal for the prize of the upward call of God in Christ Jesus (Philippians 3:12-14)."

We must forget what lies behind us to reach the goal before us. No one wins a race by watching those who are behind. A race is won by concentrating on the finish line ahead. We will not attain our prize in this life, but we won't reach it at all if we hold on to the things that hurt us. Continuing to allow our past, and the people who betrayed us, to remain in our heads and hearts allows defeat. It makes us race in vain (Philippians 2:16). Forgiving those who have wronged us is not saying what they did was okay, instead, forgiveness releases the offenses to God and allows healing.

"For if you forgive others their trespasses, your heavenly Father will also forgive you, but if you do not forgive others their trespasses, neither will your Father forgive your trespasses (Matthew 6:14-15)."

The End

"But when they went to bury her, they found no more of her than the skull and the feet and the palms of her hands. When they came back and told him, he said, 'This is the word of the Lord, which he spoke by his servant Elijah the Tishbite: In the territory of Jezreel the dogs shall eat the flesh of Jezebel, and the corpse of Jezebel shall be as dung on the face of the field in the territory of Jezreel, so that no one can say, This is Jezebel.'"
~2 Kings 9:35-37

No matter how God continued to show His love for Israel, the people continued in their rebellion. For some, it wasn't just disobedience but downright spitting in the face of God. Jezebel was one of the worst; she worshipped false gods, practiced witchcraft, and used sex as a weapon to get her own way. Not only that, she also encouraged the people she ruled to do the same. When she met her end, it was pretty gruesome. I can see the parallels between the kings and queens in the old testament and some of the leaders in our modern era who have also led the people astray; Hitler, Stalin, Clinton, Obama. There are many more of course, but all of them had one thing in common with Jezebel - they abused their position for personal gain, power, and gratification. Throughout the Old Testament, these greedy rulers meet an untimely end. God does not suffer fools forever.

"Now the works of the flesh are evident: sexual immorality, impurity, sensuality, idolatry, sorcery, enmity, strife, jealousy, fits of anger, rivalries, dissensions, divisions, envy, drunkenness, orgies, and

things like these. I warn you, as I warned you before, that those who do such things will not inherit
the kingdom of God (Galatians 5:19-21)."*

All these things practiced by Jezebel, and by
us, are of our own fleshly desires. We make decisions every day, and when we choose desires of the
flesh over rational, common sense, over what we
know is right in the eyes of God, we are bringing on
our own gruesome end. The only answer is repentance through the blood of Jesus Christ.

*"If we confess our sins, He is faithful and just to
forgive us our sins and to cleanse us from all unrighteousness (1 John 1:9)."*

*"And Peter said to them, 'Repent and be baptized
every one of you in the name of Jesus Christ for the
forgiveness of your sins, and you will receive the
gift of the Holy Spirit' (Acts 2:38)."*

There will be an end one day. Our lives do not
go on forever. We will die and step from this life
into the afterlife. We will stand before God Almighty, sinners and saints alike. Whether we believe
in God right now or not, we will all become true believers one day. The problem is, if we wait until we
stand before Him, it's too late. Our fate is sealed
the moment we exhale our last breath. Don't wait
until the end.

*"Just so, I tell you, there will be more joy in Heaven
over one sinner who repents than over ninety-nine
righteous persons who need no repentance (Luke
15:7, 10)."*

The Last Days

"But understand this, that in the last days there will come times of difficulty. For people will be lovers of self, lovers of money, proud, arrogant, abusive, dis-obedient to their parents, ungrateful, unholy, heartless, unappeasable, slanderous, without self-control, brutal, not loving good, treacherous, reckless, swollen with conceit, lovers of pleasure rather than lovers of God, having the appearance of godliness, but denying its power. Avoid such people."
~2Timothy 3:1-5

There is no doubt we live in perilous times. Every day, war in the Middle East looms closer. Terrorism, violence, crime, and all types of evil surrounds us. Those things, however, have always been with us. We are a people of war, and since Cain killed Able, we've continued that vein. We've gone from sticks, rocks, and swords to some pretty impressive weapons. Our ability to kill each other one-on-one has reached new proportions, but our ability to kill millions with the push of a button has been a real and present danger since WW2 when Hiroshima and Nagasaki were bombed. Our nuclear capabilities are endless. As a people, we are self-destructive. As a race, we are ruthless, murderous, and treacherous. As individuals, we are selfish, self-centered, egotistical, and there is no good thing within us (Romans 3:10).

"For I know that nothing good dwells in me, that is, in my flesh. For I have the desire to do what is right, but not the ability to carry it out (Romans 7:18)."

47

Our fleshly desires lead us astray. We are like monkeys who see something shiny and must have it. We chase after impossible goals in search of happiness that we never find. We throw away relationships, marriages, and children because something better and more exciting comes along. We want instant gratification and if we don't get what we want, we have no problem throwing tantrums over it or knocking someone in the head to take it. We live from the outside in, thinking external gratification will bring internal peace. Living externally only brings strife, anger, and unhappiness. We must learn to live from the inside out. No thing, no person or object, can make us happy. Happiness, contentment and peace come from within. When we learn to be happy and content, we have peace. True peace is only found in a relationship with Jesus Christ. All else is glitter.

"Finally, all of you, have unity of mind, sympathy, brotherly love, a tender heart, and a humble mind. Do not repay evil for evil or reviling for reviling, but on the contrary, bless, for to this you were called, that you may obtain a blessing. For whoever desires to love life and see good days, let him keep his tongue from evil and his lips from speaking deceit; let him turn away from evil and do good; let him seek peace and pursue it. For the eyes of the Lord are on the righteous, and His ears are open to their prayer. But the face of the Lord is against those who do evil (1 Peter 3:8-12)."

We are living in the last days, both physically and metaphorically. No one knows when their last breath will be, no one knows when the Lord will return. We can know the time is approaching by the signs we see. If we have heart problems, we can know a heart attack may be imminent; if we constantly drive like we're on a racetrack, we can know a wreck is in our future; if we drink excessively, we can know our liver is going to give out; there's ways and means to know if we are living dangerously or excessively. There are also ways and means to know that the Lord is going to return. It's not a matter of "if" but "when." Rest assured that no matter when or how you die, you will stand before the Lord God Almighty and answer for how you lived on Earth. The only answer is to always be ready.

"Therefore, God has highly exalted Him and bestowed on Him the name that is above every name, so that at the name of Jesus every knee should bow, in heaven and on Earth and under the Earth, and every tongue confess that Jesus Christ is Lord, to the glory of God the Father (Philippians 2:9-11)."

The Law of the Lord

"The law of the Lord is perfect, reviving the soul; the testimony of the Lord is sure, making wise the simple; the precepts of the Lord are right, rejoicing the heart; the commandment of the Lord is pure, enlightening the eyes; the fear of the Lord is clean, enduring forever; the rules of the Lord are true, and righteous altogether. More to be desired are they than gold, even much fine gold; sweeter also than honey and drippings of the honeycomb. Moreover, by them is your servant warned; in keeping them there is great reward."
~ Psalm 19:7-11

I love these verses because of the way they separate God's laws from the laws we currently have. The law of the Lord is perfect, sure, right, pure, clean, enduring, true, and righteous. I don't think I would describe any of the laws we have right now by those words. While I don't find it difficult to follow laws, after all, most are common sense and keep us from danger, but I do find there are way too many laws, and most are redundant. I don't think I would describe any of our laws today as pure, clean or righteous, and I wouldn't say they are desired more than gold nor are they sweeter than honey.

That's the difference between God's laws and man's laws. Man's laws are designed to be followed under penalty of fines or imprisonment; God's laws are designed to be followed out of love and for blessings. However, I see the reasoning and necessity of man's laws, and until everyone is under the subjection of Jesus Christ, those laws will continue to be a necessity.

"For this is the love of God, that we keep His commandments. And His commandments are not burdensome. For everyone who has been born of God overcomes the world. And this is the victory that has overcome the world—our faith (1 John 5:3-4)."

We don't obey God because of fear of penalty but out of love for what He has done for us. Those of us who lived a life of sin or have been on the wrong side of man's law, know that following the Lord is easy in comparison. When we accept Christ as our Savior, His laws are written on our hearts and put into our minds by the Holy Spirit (Hebrews 10:16). We don't have to try to obey, we don't have to try and be "good". We are brought into a life lived out of love and joy because we know where we were, and where we were headed before we knew the love and peace of Christ. If you are having a hard time keeping up with the laws of man, give your life and heart over to the Lord, His burden is light and easy to bear (Matthew 11:30).

"For the kingdom of God is not a matter of eating and drinking but of righteousness and peace and joy in the Holy Spirit. Whoever thus serves Christ is acceptable to God and approved by men (Romans 14:17-18)."

Rich Man vs. Poor Man

"But Abraham said, 'Child, remember that you in your lifetime received your good things, and Lazarus in like manner bad things; but now he is comforted here, and you are in anguish."
~Luke 16:25

Luke 16:19-31 tells the story of "a certain" rich man, and Lazarus, a poor man, who both died. The rich man had a life of luxury, while Lazarus suffered his entire life with some sort of disease that made him unable to work and had to beg for food. They both died and verse 22 says that Lazarus was carried away by angels, while the rich man was buried and tormented in Hades. Lazarus, on the other hand, was comforted by Abraham. The rich man could see that Lazarus and Abraham had quite a different afterlife than he did, but no matter how he tried to bargain, the rich man could not cross over to Abraham. He could not change his fate. He finally tried to convince Abraham to allow Lazarus to be raised from the dead in order to tell the rich man's five brothers what awaited them in death but that wasn't allowed either. *"He said to him, 'If they do not hear Moses and the Prophets, neither will they be convinced if someone should rise from the dead (v. 31).'"*
Although wealth does not preclude one from going to Heaven, and poverty does not guarantee Heaven for anyone; I was struck by verse 31 for one reason, someone did rise from the dead—Jesus Christ. He was seen by hundreds of people and walked the Earth for forty days after He rose from the dead, yet people still refuse to believe the Bible as truth for their lives, both then and now. We have

the evidence of Creation all around us. We have the Word of God, we have churches everywhere, and TV and radio stations full of gospel broadcasts, yet people continue to scoff at the idea Jesus Christ can change their lives and eternal destiny.

"For since the creation of the world God's invisible qualities—His eternal power and divine nature—have been clearly seen, being understood from what has been made, so that people are without excuse (Romans 1:20)."

We are without excuse when it comes to salvation and eternity. We have all the evidence necessary to know and understand who God is and what He did on the Cross through the body of Jesus Christ. We make the choice for Heaven or hell every day by choosing whether we will follow Christ or go our own way. For many of us, we were absolutely convinced that our way was not working, and we had only one choice: choose Jesus or die. For others, perhaps the choice is more difficult because they do have money that allows for their bad behavior, allows them to get out of whatever trouble they find, and allows them to go through life as if their behavior has no real consequences. It does seem that way when we read the news about celebrities or politicians getting away with things that a normal person would be in prison for.

"Do not lay up for yourselves treasures on Earth, where moth and rust destroy and where thieves break in and steal, but lay up for yourselves treasures in heaven, where neither moth nor rust destroys and where thieves do not break in and

steal. For where your treasure is, there your heart will be also (Matthew 6:19-21)."

Our hearts are our moral compass. Whatever direction it's pointed to is where our lives follow, and it's sad to think that while Creation praises the work of God's hand, His greatest Creation – us – continues to deny Him.

"He is the image of the invisible God, the firstborn of all creation. For by Him all things were created, in Heaven and on Earth, visible and invisible, whether thrones or dominions or rulers or authorities—all things were created through Him and for Him. And He is before all things, and in Him all things hold together. And He is the head of the body, the church. He is the beginning, the firstborn from the dead, that in everything He might be preeminent. For in Him all the fullness of God was pleased to dwell, and through Him to reconcile to Himself all things, whether on Earth or in Heaven, making peace by the blood of His Cross (Colossians 1:15-20)."

Crossing Lines

"If then you have been raised with Christ, seek the things that are above, where Christ is, seated at the right hand of God. Set your minds on things that are above, not on things that are on Earth. For you have died, and your life is hidden with Christ in God. When Christ who is your life appears, then you also will appear with Him in glory."
~Colossians 3:1-4

I was thinking about lines the other day while driving down the road on the big truck with my husband. Our entire lives are dictated by lines—lines on the roads we drive, lines at the businesses we patronize, lines we can see and those we can't. "Girl, you've crossed the line this time," was my dad's favorite saying. When I was younger, that always confused me because I had no idea what line he was talking about. However, as I got older, I crossed so many lines that if they were visible, the path behind me would look like some artist went crazy!

However, for the past 35+ years, I've walked a relatively straight line, doing what I'm supposed to do and being the kind of woman that makes God proud. Don't get me wrong, I still cross lines that perhaps other people don't approve of, and I say things that tend to shock people, but I'm a plain-spoken person. I don't mince words or say things just to make people feel better. And mostly, I do not care what people think about me; I am not in this world to please people. I am here to please God by serving others, which I sincerely try to do every single day. Do I feel as if I do that every day? Absolutely not. But I get up every morning and start over again because my hope lies within Jesus Christ, not within my own capabilities.

"Put to death therefore what is Earthly in you: sexual immorality, impurity, passion, evil desire, and covetousness, which is idolatry. On account of these the wrath of God is coming. In these you too once walked, when you were living in them. But now you must put them all away: anger, wrath, malice, slander, and obscene talk from your mouth. Do not lie to one another, seeing that you have put off the old self with its practices and have put on the new self, which is being renewed in knowledge after the image of its Creator. Here there is not Greek and Jew, circumcised and uncircumcised, barbarian, Scythian, slave, free; but Christ is all, and in all (Colossians 3:5-11)."

"In these too you once walked..." We all walk in evil ways until we come to the knowledge of who Christ is and what He can do to change our lives, and then we put off *"the old self,"* which is our sinful ways, and *"put on the new self,"* which is Christ in us. It doesn't seem possible at times that Christ could possibly love us even in our sins and want us to be part of His heavenly Kingdom. When we know how wrong our lives are, how wrong our thinking is, how wrong our hearts are, it seems impossible that life can change into something wonderful and worthwhile.

I think about Christ on the Cross and the moment everything went dark for three hours (Mark 15:33). That was the moment Father God turned away. That was the moment Christ knew what it was like to be a sinner because every sin that could ever be committed was fully on Him. Christ, the perfect, sinless Lamb of God, knew exactly what it was like to cross every line we could ever imagine, and some we can't. God cannot look on sin, and because His Son was covered in our filth, He looked away and darkness fell. That's what sin is—pure darkness. It covers our hearts and minds and prevents us from seeing that which is pure light.

Imagine life as a two-lane road, with a broken white line down the middle. Anyone who's ever driven a car knows that a solid line is one you can't cross to pass other cars; you have to wait for the broken line. Our lives are one big line too, and we choose which lane we're going to travel in. Sin is the solid line that keeps us in one lane but when we are broken and come to the knowledge that sin is killing us, it's then that we can cross that line into the arms of Jesus Christ.

"Put on then, as God's chosen ones, holy and beloved, compassionate hearts, kindness, humility, meekness, and patience, bearing with one another and, if one has a complaint against another, forgiving each other; as the Lord has forgiven you, so you also must forgive. And above all these, put on love, which binds everything together in perfect harmony. And let the peace of Christ rule in your hearts, to which indeed you were called in one body. And be thankful. Let the word of Christ dwell in you richly, teaching and admonishing one another in all wisdom, singing psalms and hymns and spiritual songs, with thankfulness in your hearts to God. And whatever you do, in word or deed, do everything in the name of the Lord Jesus, giving thanks to God the Father through Him (Colossians 3:12-17)."

Old Cars

"For thus says the High and Lofty One who inhabits eternity, whose name is Holy: 'I dwell in the high and holy place, with him who has a contrite and humble spirit, to revive the spirit of the humble, and to revive the heart of the contrite ones.'"
~Psalm 57:15

I love old cars. There's just something about the rounded fenders, bulky bodies, and roomy interiors that appeals to me. Unlike today's cars that are all so generic, you can't tell one model from another. My favorite car is a 1957 Chevy. I often see old cars sitting in yards or lots, they're rusted out with flat tires and oxidized paint. They look terrible and it makes me sad because I know what they looked like when they came off the assembly line. But every now and then, I'll see one in someone's driveway on blocks being restored, and it gives me a thrill to know that car is going to be shiny and beautiful again.

We're kind of like those old cars—no matter how we exercise or eat right, we still age and our bodies break down. We're really just a bunch of old Chevy's in the junkyard of life. But we have an advantage, we don't have to sit and rust, we can be recycled into someone shiny and new, too.

There's a lot of stress and pressure in today's world, and it's easy to feel like a generic model that looks, dresses, and acts like every other model around us. Striving to be noticed can be a lot of unnecessary work when our goal is to impress someone like a boss, or someone else we feel has a higher station in life than we do. On every level, the world says we have to be better than someone else, we have to earn more, have more, be more, do more, and if we don't, there's something wrong with us and we're not worth noticing. We even get caught up with that idea in our own heads, setting goals that we can't attain and then beat ourselves up because we can't. It causes discourse in every area of life and leads to a myriad of health problems like high blood pressure, but it also leads to mental health problems like depression and suicide.

A recent report states that 13% of the population ages 12 and over is taking antidepressants, and 68% of those have taken the drugs for ten years or longer. However, that number is small compared to the 94% of the population who report having stress related health problems.

"Come to Me, all who labor and are heavy laden, and I will give you rest. Take My yoke upon you, and learn from Me, for I am gentle and lowly in heart, and you will find rest for your souls. For My yoke is easy, and My burden is light (Matthew 11:28-30)."

Yokes aren't used much these days but in ancient times, they were heavy wooden implements that were used to team up oxen for heavy work, like plowing, pulling wagons, and other work that was too much for a human being. Stress and worry are a yoke that is too much for humans to bear. We all need rest, not just physical rest but mental rest. When we get mentally weary, we begin to lose hope and that's when depression sets in. It can come from doing too much, worrying too much, berating ourselves for not achieving what we think we should, from taking the words of others to heart, and from having unrealistic expectations. But Jesus says if we come to Him, He will give us that rest.

First, we must come to Him. That means we accept who He is as being absolute truth. Second, we take His yoke upon us, or we exchange yokes. Ours is heavy and wearisome, His is light and easy. Third, we learn from Him. Exchanging our knowledge of this life for His knowledge is a burden-lifting, stress-reducing, spirit-elevating event that leaves us feeling freer than we ever have before. Jesus can take any old jalopy and make it brand new again!

"Peace I leave with you; My peace I give to you. Not as the world gives do I give to you. Let not your hearts be troubled, neither let them be afraid (John 14:27)."

When God Hears Me

"We know that God does not listen to sinners, but if anyone is a worshiper of God and does His will, God listens to him."
~John 9:31

While researching today's topic, I ran across a post by a young lady who read this verse and said she was now "scared" because everything she had read about God was that He loves us, so if this verse is true, she didn't know what would happen to her soul when she died. Honestly, I kind of chuckled over the post but as I began to think about her words, it occurred to me that she's really confused over who God is, what He's all about and why Jesus came to Earth.

Many years ago, someone told me of a vision (attributed to Rick Joyner, however, I can't confirm) about prayers being arrows shot toward Heaven. The prayers of the saints (those who know Jesus as their Savior) were collected by an angel and put into his quiver, but those prayed by sinners where deflected by the angel's shield and sent hurling into space. That analogy has stuck with me all this time, and it illustrates the verse in John. God hears our prayers when we 1) have accepted Christ as our Savior 2) pray with right motives 3) pray according to His will 4) our prayers line up with Scripture.

"You desire and do not have, so you murder. You covet and cannot obtain, so you fight and quarrel. You do not have, because you do not ask. You ask and do not receive, because you ask wrongly, to spend it on your passions. You adulterous people! Do

you not know that friendship with the world is enmity with God? Therefore, whoever wishes to be a friend of the world makes himself an enemy of God (James 4:2-4)."

It's been my experience that enemies don't want to do things for you. In fact, enemies don't want you involved in their lives in any way at all. When we choose to live in the world, with all its corruption, we are telling God that we choose to be His enemy. Yet, when things go wrong, we still want God to fix it for us, or we want to blame Him. You can't ride two horses with one saddle, folks. You either choose the world and all its lusts, or you choose God and all His blessings. You can't have it both ways. When you choose an action, you are also choosing the consequences. Follow the ways of this world, you go to hell. Follow Jesus Christ and you reap His many blessings, including Heaven.

"So put away all malice and all deceit and hypocrisy and envy and all slander. Like newborn infants, long for the pure spiritual milk, that by it you may grow up into salvation—if indeed you have tasted that the Lord is good. As you come to him, a living stone rejected by men but in the sight of God chosen and precious, you yourselves like living stones are being built up as a spiritual house, to be a holy priesthood, to offer spiritual sacrifices acceptable to God through Jesus Christ (1 Peter 2:1-5)."

1) Accept Christ as your Savior
2) Pray with right motives
3) Pray according to God's will
4) Align your heart with Scripture, the heart of God

When people try to walk the fence between this world and a life with Christ, they are going to fall, and usually, it's on the side of the world. We must make choices in life every single day, and that includes life and death, Heaven or hell, Jesus or satan. When you choose the world, you are choosing death, hell, and satan. God loves us, He is always waiting on us to choose Him, but until we do, our prayers will not be answered.

Barking Dogs

"Repay no one evil for evil but give thought to do what is honorable in the sight of all. If possible, so far as it depends on you, live peaceably with all."
~Romans 12:17-18

When we moved to help my daughter with her children, we lived with her family and later, before we bought our cabin in the mountains, we got a house near them. I never liked living in town and it's been an adjustment having moved from our little farm on 400 acres. My dogs like it even less than I do. They have been able to run, go swimming, and hunt rabbits and deer all their lives. Now, they are inside most of the time and when they go out, it's to a tiny yard. They aren't used to the noise, the cars, the kids screaming as they ride their bikes, or other dogs barking in the distance. Frankly, neither am I.

The topper came when someone called the cops because my dogs were barking while I was gone, and the Chief of Police came out to chat. I'm sure he had better things to do than talk to me about barking dogs but at least he was nice. Of course, he didn't tell me who called but I have an idea. Everything in me wants to go knock on a door and ask but I'm an adult, and it wasn't really a big deal in the light of day. What bothers me most is that they could have waited until I was home and came to talk to me. That's how we handle things back home.

"Strive for peace with everyone, and for the holiness without which no one will see the Lord. See to it that no one fails to obtain the grace of God; that no "root of bitterness" springs up and causes

trouble, and by it many become defiled (Hebrews 12:14-15)."

It's not easy to live with humans, especially when we are forced to live in such close proximity that we can hear everything they do. We know when they go to work, when they get home, what time they cook dinner, and everything else that goes on. Humans are noisy, messy, busybodies that can't walk to the mailbox without checking out other houses on the way. Trying to live peaceably among other people is something we have yet to achieve, but it is something we are instructed to do.

I had to exercise a lot of patience when living in town. The things I wasn't used to, like people, traffic, lawnmowers and weed eaters running from morning to night, make me want to run back home. Instead, I have adopted a practice of telling myself, "Practice patience, practice patience, practice patience," as many times as necessary until I'm either calm or start laughing at the ridiculousness of the situation. Because we all know that hot tempers cause arguments, but patience brings peace (Proverbs 15:18).

"But the fruit of the Spirit is love, joy, peace, patience, kindness, goodness, faithfulness, gentleness, self-control; against such things there is no law. And those who belong to Christ Jesus have crucified the flesh with its passions and desires. If we live by the Spirit, let us also keep in step with the Spirit. Let us not become conceited, provoking one another, envying one another (Galatians 5:22-26)."

Where's The Rewind Button?

"Let love be genuine. Abhor what is evil; hold fast to what is good. Love one another with brotherly affection. Outdo one another in showing honor."
~Romans 12:9-10

There is no respect left in this world. When I was a kid, we were taught to respect ourselves, others, especially our elders, and those who were less fortunate than us. We didn't talk back to our parents, at least not without getting our mouths slapped, we behaved in school, and we didn't make fun of people who were different either in dress, culture, or because of disabilities. I raised my kids to be respectful of others and to keep their thoughts to themselves. No matter if they liked what someone wore, said or did, they were taught that just because you disagree with someone, doesn't mean you have to call them names or make them feel stupid. Not so in today's world.

I feel like I've stepped through the looking glass into a parody of the world I grew up in, even the world my kids grew up in. The world my grandchildren are growing up in is so foreign to me that I'm not sure how to navigate it. And I certainly don't like it. We are all in this thing called life together. We have the same basic needs, wants and desires. We have the same hopes, dreams, and fears. Yet, to me, it seems as if everything is just a little off kilter, like it's all tipped sideways and I don't know how to set it upright, or if it's even possible to be set upright.

Jesus Christ teaches us to love one another, to respect each other, and to show that love and respect openly by honoring one another in all that we say and do. He teaches us to care for the poor, weak, and less fortunate, and to be generous to those in need. He teaches that a kind word goes a lot farther than a harsh one, and that love covers a multitude of sin (1 Peter 4:8).

Philippians 2:4
Let each of you look not only to his own interests, but also to the interests of others.

Ephesians 4:32
Be kind to one another, tenderhearted, forgiving one another, as God in Christ forgave you.

John 13:34-35
A new commandment I give to you, that you love one another: just as I have loved you, you also are to love one another. By this all people will know that you are my disciples, if you have love for one another."

1 John 3:17-18
But if anyone has the world's goods and sees his brother in need, yet closes his heart against him, how does God's love abide in him? Little children, let us not love in word or talk but in deed and in truth.

Proverbs 21:13
Whoever closes his ear to the cry of the poor will himself call out and not be answered.

1 Timothy 5:8
But if anyone does not provide for his relatives, and especially for members of his household, he has denied the faith and is worse than an unbeliever.

Galatians 6:9-10
And let us not grow weary of doing good, for in due season we will reap, if we do not give up. So then, as we have opportunity, let us do good to everyone, and especially to those who are of the household of faith.

Matthew 25:40
And the King will answer them, 'Truly, I say to you, as you did it to one of the least of these my brothers, you did it to me.'

1 Thessalonians 5:11
Therefore encourage one another and build one another up, just as you are doing.

Proverbs 28:27
Whoever gives to the poor will not want, but he who hides his eyes will get many a curse.

I want to hit the rewind button and go back to a simpler time when the world made sense but when I look backwards, I can see how the world was headed toward the way it is today all along. There is no going back, all we can do is govern ourselves, our mouths, our actions, and look to the Lord for guidance and comfort, and pray for the day He returns to set it all right again.

Loss & Grief

"His delight is not in the strength of the horse, nor
His pleasure in the legs of a man, but the Lord takes
pleasure in those who fear Him, in those who hope
in His steadfast love."
~Psalm 147:10-11

There are certain times in our lives when we reflect on the events of life that have defined us—some good, some not so good but no matter what they are, they have been the game changers for us. I've had a lot of those in my life and I've learned to make sense of most of them and then put them away in the "over and done with" file in my mind. On occasion, something will come up that cracks that file open and like rubberneckers at a car wreck, I have to go back and take a look—even when good sense is telling me to slam that drawer shut and walk away. I still have to look and pick at a scab until it bleeds again. Even though I know I'd be better off not rehashing those things, it's part of the grief process.

We grieve over the things we've lost in life even if we don't realize it, and grief, while it lessens with time, never really stops. It's an ongoing process that can come up at any time and if we don't recognize it for what it is, we can experience waves of varied emotions from depression to anger. Learning to deal with grief is a lifelong process but first, we must recognize it for what it is and accept that we must go through the process in order to walk out the other side. Getting stuck in grief is not a good place to be and has its own consequences that can be terminal and lead to mental disorders, complete breakdowns, and suicide.

Elisabeth Kubler Ross defined the stages of grief as 1) denial 2) anger 3) bargaining 4) depression 5) acceptance. These stages help us put a name to what we are feeling when we experience loss, whether the loss of a loved one, the loss of a job, lifestyle, home, marriage, or anything that was part of who we are and what we believed defined us. There is no timeline for any of the stages, and often we feel more than one at a time. We can also go from one stage to another and then back again. There is no "order" or amount of time that is "normal" for any particular stage of the grieving process.

Sometimes, especially when things seem to be going well and we think we've got a handle on our emotions, and we've pulled ourselves through the going through, we can suddenly be pulled back into one of the stages of grief. A loss experienced by someone we know, a particular date, a certain place, or even the wafting of a scent on the air can hurtle us back in time to our own place of grief.

We can suddenly be back in the grieving process, flooded with emotions we thought we had dealt with. Recognizing what we are feeling and why is important to walking through each emotion and being able to put it back into the "over and done with" file. This can take days or weeks, or even longer, but as long as we are processing the feelings and not getting stuck in them, we are on the right track.

It is important, whether it's you or someone you know, who is experiencing grief, to know how to help. 1) Acknowledge the reason for your emotions 2) Talk to someone or be an active listener—advice is not always necessary or welcome but having someone really listen can be one of the greatest helps

3) Don't isolate—being alone in your own mind can be a dangerous place to hang out. Being present for someone else can be all they need as well. 4) Understand that grieving can be a long process and there is no time limit on emotions, yours or someone else's. 5) Understand that grief emotions can come up at any time. There is no correlation between the amount of time since the loss occurred and the current emotions.

"Blessed be the God and Father of our Lord Jesus Christ, the Father of mercies and God of all comfort, who comforts us in all our affliction, so that we may be able to comfort those who are in any affliction, with the comfort with which we ourselves are comforted by God (2 Corinthians 1:3-4)."

Platitudes

*"For I was hungry, and you gave me food, I was
thirsty, and you gave me drink, I was a stranger and
you welcomed me, I was naked, and you clothed
me, I was sick, and you visited me, I was in prison
and you came to me.' Then the righteous will answer him, saying, 'Lord, when did we see you hungry
and feed you, or thirsty and give you drink? And
when did we see you a stranger and welcome you, or
naked and clothe you? And when did we see you sick
or in prison and visit you?' And the King will answer
them, 'Truly, I say to you, as you did it to one of
the least of these my brothers, you did it to me.'"*
~Matthew 25:35-40

Recently, I found myself questioning how I re-
sponded to the needs of others due to a particular
incident. I had talked with someone about the incident and their response was, "I'll pray for you."
Now, as Christians, that's a pretty pat answer, and
while praying for others is of vital importance, it's
not all we should, or could, do. I actually wanted a
little more in regard to an answer and felt let down
that all the other person could offer was "I'll pray
for you." It sounded like platitudes.

Jesus was practical in all that He did. While
prayer was a part of His life, when it came to others,
it wasn't all He did. In John 4 there is a story about
the Samaritan woman at the well. Jesus didn't look
at her and say, "I'll pray for you," and continue on
His way. First, He engaged her in conversation, sec-
ondly, He addressed her needs, and third, He revealed Himself to her.

In John 6, the crowds had been around Jesus for a long time, it was the Passover and time to eat. Jesus didn't tell people to go home and grab a bite to eat. First, He addressed their need, second, He provided for that need, and third, He prayed about the need.

In John 11, Lazarus was ill, so his sisters sent for Jesus to help him. By the time Jesus arrived, Lazarus had died. First, Jesus acknowledged the need, second, He gave the people around the tomb hope, third, He raised Lazarus from the dead. There are many more instances of how Jesus helped those in need by being practical and addressing the need in whatever way would glorify God and point to Himself as the Savior of the world. The application of what Jesus did for others is a lesson for us in how to address the needs of others: 1) Assess the need 2) Address the need 3) Pray about the need.

Jesus also listened to people and engaged them in conversation. He found out what they needed and found a way to help them that wasn't gratuitous but instead, life changing. We can give money to charities for the poor, donate clothing to an outreach, and say we will pray for someone but how life-changing are those acts? Are we actually helping and pointing someone to Christ? Or are we just making ourselves feel better? I have been guilty of this very thing. I have given money, donated clothing, and said, "I'll pray for you." But what did those things really do, other than make me feel better about myself?

When someone is in need, whether physically or emotionally, we have a greater duty than to say, "I'll pray for you." We have a duty to our Savior to emulate Him and offer practical solutions for any given situation.

"But be doers of the word, and not hearers only, deceiving yourselves. For if anyone is a hearer of the word and not a doer, he is like a man who looks intently at his natural face in a mirror. For he looks at himself and goes away and at once forgets what he was like. But the one who looks into the perfect law, the law of liberty, and perseveres, being no hearer who forgets but a doer who acts, he will be blessed in his doing (James 1:22-25)."

Lift Your Eyes

"Do not fear, for I have redeemed you; I have called you by name, you are Mine. When you pass through the waters, I will be with you; and through the rivers, they shall not overwhelm you; when you walk through fire you shall not be burned, and the flame shall not consume you. For I am the Lord you God, the Holy One of Israel, your Savior."
~Isaiah 43:1-3

There are times in life when we are tired, worn out, and drained. Sometimes, we need to take a step back and recharge. I find being alone with God is the best way to do that. I turn on my favorite worship music, I dance and sing and praise God. I read the Bible and I pray. I watch videos of my favorite teachings from Rabbi Schneider and Pastor Irvin Baxter. Not always in that order. I am a visual person and an interactive person. I like being able to express myself in whatever way fills my heart and soul with the peace that can only come from a holy Lord. Worshipping Jesus Christ for who He is and what He's done in my life gives me the peace that surpasses all understanding. No matter what goes on in life, I know I can count on Him.

"I lift up my eyes to the hills. From where does my help come? My help comes from the Lord, who made Heaven and Earth. He will not let your foot be moved; He who keeps you will not slumber. Behold, He who keeps Israel will neither slumber nor sleep. The Lord is your keeper; the Lord is your shade on your right hand. The sun shall not strike you by day,

nor the moon by night. The Lord will keep you from all evil; He will keep your life. The Lord will keep your going out and your coming in from this time forth and forevermore (Psalm 121)."

God's promises never change. They are the same today as they were yesterday, and they'll be the same tomorrow as they are today. No matter what happens in life, or how we feel, or how tired we get, the Lord is still on our side. He is still our advocate in a world that tries to tear us down. He is our peace when the oceans rage and the volcanoes flow into the sea. He is our comfort when the Earth shakes, and the winds spin out of control. He is always with us no matter what is going on in life, or even when life is smooth as glass. Our only job is to accept His great love and love Him in return. Jesus Christ showed His great love for us when He died on the Cross (John 15:13); we show ours in our worship, prayer and Bible study.

"By this we shall know that we are of the truth and reassure our heart before Him; for whenever our heart condemns us, God is greater than our heart, and He knows everything (1 John 3:19-20)."

Counting Joy

"Count it all joy, my brothers, when you meet trials of various kinds, for you know that the testing of your faith produces steadfastness. And let steadfastness have its full effect, that you may be perfect and complete, lacking in nothing."
~James 1:2-4

Life is full of unavoidable trials. People are going to let us down, break our hearts, and disappoint us. Some events in life are going to make us doubt and question what we are doing and why. We don't have control over what other people do, and we can't always be in control of events that occur in our lives, but how we deal with situations is within our control.

Counting the trials of life as joy seems to be a contradiction, but when we read the above verse in context, it isn't the trial but the result of the trial that we count as joy. Trials test us, our faith, and our character. The result of the trials in life is that it makes us stronger, increases our faith, and draws us closer to God. Even circumstances that feel as if they will break us serves a higher purpose. Withstanding trials doesn't mean we can't cry, feel anger, depression, or doubt while going through them.

Some people think that being a Christian means never wavering or expressing any of the emotions that come naturally but Christ expressed all those emotions in His life. He was angry with the money changers (Matthew 21:12); He was moved to compassion (Luke 7:12-15); He showed great love (John 13:23); His heart was broken when Judas be trayed Him (Mark 14:10-72); He was abandoned (Matthew 26:56); He experienced doubt on His way to the Cross (Matthew 26:39); He felt agony when being whipped and beaten, and suffered physical and mental pain while on the Cross; and He gave up hope when God turned away from the sin laid upon Him (John 19). Yet, through everything He suffered, Jesus did not sin (1 Peter 2:22), and instead of hating those who had tortured and hurt Him, He asked God to forgive them (Luke 23:34).

"Count it all joy, my brothers, when you meet trials of various kinds, for you know that the testing of your faith produces steadfastness. And let steadfastness have its full effect, that you may be perfect and complete, lacking in nothing (James 1:2-4)."

Steadfastness literally means "fixed in place but is chiefly used figuratively to indicate undeviating constancy or resolution, as in steadfast faith." We can be steadfast in our faith no matter what we are going through in life because of all the things Jesus went through for our salvation.

"Little children, you are from God and have overcome them, for He who is in you is greater than he who is in the world (1 John 4:4)."

Blessed Be The Name of the Lord

"Then Job arose and tore his robe and shaved his head and fell on the ground and worshiped. And he said, 'Naked I came from my mother's womb, and naked shall I return. The Lord gave, and the Lord has taken away; blessed be the name of the Lord.' In all this Job did not sin or charge God with wrong."
~Job 1:20-22

It doesn't take many years on this planet to figure out that life isn't fair. In fact, life is down-right unfair and it's a lifelong struggle to get through. Life hurts us mentally and physically, and from time to time, can leave us gasping in the dirt trying to figure out what happened and what's going on. The one thing that's certain is life won't leave any of us unscathed; but how we handle life's distress, disasters, and disappointments is totally up to us.

I think it's why I like reading the Book of Job so much. The devil unleashed his worst on Job, yet through everything he endured, Job *"did not sin or charge God with wrong."* As a chaplain, I have heard many people blame God for what is wrong in their lives, even people who claim to not believe in God, blame Him when things go wrong. I have also had many people ask, "Why would God allow this to happen?" Answering people who blame God is much easier than answering why He allows things to happen.

In my own life I have endured many losses from the death of a daughter to the death of grandchildren and a husband. I have watched my father battle cancer, as well as having many friends who have either had cancer or had a loved one with

cancer. I've grieved with others who have had simi-
lar losses in their lives, and I've stayed awake many
nights praying for an answer to "why?" In truth, I
don't know why God allows the things that happen
to us, especially to those who serve Him in everything they do. Yes, it does seem unfair to me; yes, it
does hurt to think that God isn't as concerned as I
think He should be; but no, I do not blame God because I believe the Bible.

"Likewise, the Spirit helps us in our weakness.
For we do not know what to pray for as we ought,
but the Spirit Himself intercedes for us with groan-
ings too deep for words. And He who searches hearts
knows what is the mind of the Spirit because the
Spirit intercedes for the saints according to the will
of God. And we know that for those who love God
all things work together for good, for those who are
called according to His purpose. For those whom
He foreknew He also predestined to be conformed
to the image of His Son, in order that He might
be the firstborn among many brothers. And those
whom He predestined He also called, and those
whom He called He also justified, and those whom
He justified He also glorified (Romans 8:25-30)."

When we are called by God, we know who we
are in Him. We know that no matter what happens in
life, it is a temporary situation. We know that what
happens here on Earth strengthens and refines us
and conforms us to the image of Christ. We know
that there is a better plan, an ultimate plan laid out
for us by God before we were even created in the
womb (Jeremiah 1:5), and the God who planned for
us to be born will never forget or abandon us (He-

brews 13:5). We are His and He has written our names on the palm of His hand (Isaiah 49:16). There is nothing we go through that God has not already prepared a conclusion for us. So, if the odds are rigged, they are definitely in our favor!

The story of Job is a life lesson for us all. Yes, there will be great losses and great grief. Yes, our friends will turn on us, and even our families will abandon us. We will be betrayed in ways we don't expect or see coming. We will shed tears, feel like life's biggest loser, and sometimes we will be tempted to give up and walk away. But in all things, we must remember that God is in control and He is our ever-present help in times of trouble (Psalm 46:1).

I have had to repeat Job's line many times in my life, *"The Lord gives and the Lord takes away, blessed be the Name of the Lord."* I hope this gives you encouragement no matter what you may be going through right now. It's okay to cry and be discouraged, and it's okay to grieve our losses, but we also must remember that God still has our best interest at heart and in the end, He will make all things right again.

"The Lord your God is in your midst, a mighty one who will save; He will rejoice over you with gladness; He will quiet you by his love; He will exult over you with loud singing (Zephaniah 3:17)."

Mercy & Grace

"Since then we have a great High Priest who has passed through the heavens, Jesus, the Son of God, let us hold fast our confession. For we do not have a High Priest who is unable to sympathize with our weaknesses, but One who in every respect has been tempted as we are, yet without sin. Let us then with confidence draw near to the throne of grace, that we may receive mercy and find grace to help in time of need."
~Hebrews 4:14-16

Mercy is defined as compassion or forgiveness shown toward someone whom it is within one's power to punish or harm. Grace is the free and un-merited favor of God. As humans, we don't really deserve mercy or grace. We have failed God on such a grand scale, yet He continues to show mercy by allowing the world to continue because He knows there are still those out there who will come to accept His grace through Jesus Christ.

God shows us mercy by not destroying us when He has every right to, and He shows us grace by forgiving us for everything we've done and giving us everlasting life in Heaven. It is His great compassion for us that allowed Christ to come to Earth and die for our sins. It is His great compassion that allows us to be forgiven and live a life we don't really deserve. But one day, God's mercy and grace will come to an end and instead of being our salvation, He will be our judge.

My pastor in California used to tell the following story that shows the difference between Savior and Judge:

*One day a man was driving to work and saw a car
had plunged over the railing into a creek and was
filling with water. A teenage boy was trapped in the
vehicle, struggling to free himself as the water rose
around him. The man jumped the railing, slid down
the bank and plunged into the freezing water. He
was able to break the window and cut the seatbelt,
freeing the teenager. He dragged the boy to safety
and stayed with him until help arrived. Many years
later, the teenager had become a man and broke
the law. He was arrested and brought to court. He
immediately recognized the man on the bench as
the same man who had dragged him from his car all
those years ago. He said, "Don't you remember me?
When I wrecked my car all those years ago, you
were the one who saved me!" The man looked at
the prisoner and nodded. "Yes, I do remember you.
But then, I was your savior. Today, I'm your judge."*

*"But now the righteousness of God has been mani-
fested apart from the law, although the Law and
the Prophets bear witness to it—the righteousness of
God through faith in Jesus Christ for all who believe. For there is no distinction: for all have sinned
and fall short of the glory of God, and are justified by His grace as a gift, through the redemption
that is in Christ Jesus (Romans 3:21-24)."*

Today, Jesus Christ is our Savior, full of mercy
and grace. One day we will stand before Him, and
He will be our Judge. We have only this lifetime to
do one thing right, and that's to ensure our eternal
destination is in Heaven. That is why God showers us
with such great compassion despite the things we
have done. That is why Christ died on the Cross at

Calvary. It is not God's desire that any should perish, but that all should come to salvation (2 Peter 3:9). He has done all He can to provide for our salvation and the rest is up to us. God loves us so much, He died for us in the person of Jesus Christ. God loves us, but it is up to us to love Him back.

"And you were dead in the trespasses and sins in which you once walked, following the course of this world, following the prince of the power of the air, the spirit that is now at work in the sons of disobedience—among whom we all once lived in the passions of our flesh, carrying out the desires of the body and the mind, and were by nature children of wrath, like the rest of mankind. But God, being rich in mercy, because of the great love with which He loved us, even when we were dead in our trespasses, made us alive together with Christ—by grace you have been saved—and raised us up with Him and seated us with Him in the heavenly places in Christ Jesus, so that in the coming ages He might show the immeasurable riches of His grace in kindness toward us in Christ Jesus. For by grace you have been saved through faith. And this is not your own doing; it is the gift of God, not a result of works, so that no one may boast. For we are His workmanship, created in Christ Jesus for good works, which God prepared beforehand, that we should walk in them (Ephesians 2:1-10)."

Restoration

"I will bless the Lord at all times; His praise shall continually be in my mouth. My soul makes its boast in the Lord; let the humble hear and be glad. Oh, magnify the Lord with me and let us exalt His Name together! I sought the Lord, and He answered me and delivered me from all my fears. Those who look to Him are radiant, and their faces shall never be ashamed. This poor man cried, and the Lord heard him and saved him out of all his troubles. The angel of the Lord encamps around those who fear Him and delivers them. Oh, taste and see that the Lord is good! Blessed is the man who takes refuge in Him! Oh, fear the Lord, you His saints, for those who fear Him have no lack! The young lions suffer want and hunger; but those who seek the Lord lack no good thing."
~Psalm 34:1-10

King David wrote most of the Psalms. He was a man with problems, but he was also a man with great faith and love for the Lord. It's true that most of his problems were brought on by his own fleshly desires and failure to obey the word of God, but David was also teachable. No matter what he went through, David was able to see the Lord's hand in every aspect of his life. Even when David was pursued by his enemies, lost children, or committed sins that grieved God's heart, he never failed to acknowledge His wrongs and confess his sins to God. David had a contrite spirit and knew that God would answer and forgive him. That doesn't mean God didn't allow David to suffer the consequences of his actions, but God never abandoned him.

How many times in life have we grieved the heart of God, but instead of confessing that sin, kept going in the wrong direction? That is one ploy the devil uses to lure us farther from God. If we begin to think that our sins are too great, or that we've sinned too often, or that God must be getting tired of hearing our excuses, then the devil has us right where he wants us. And the further we get from God, the closer we get to hell.

Paul called himself the "chief of sinners" (1 Timothy 1:15), and Isaiah said, "woe is me, I have unclean lips" (Isaiah 6:5). David cried out, "I have sinned against you" (Psalm 51:4), and the tax collector said, "I am a sinner" (Luke 18:13). In every case in the Bible where someone admitted their sin, God forgave and restored them to a point better than they were prior to sinning. That's because once we admit our sin and ask forgiveness, God doesn't remember that we sinned (Isaiah 43:25). We are brand new, like a newborn baby, before Him. We are innocent in His eyes and forgiven of everything we have done.

"Repent therefore, and turn back, that your sins may be blotted out, that times of refreshing may come from the presence of the Lord, and that he may send the Christ appointed for you, Jesus, whom Heaven must receive until the time for restoring all the things about which God spoke by the mouth of His holy prophets long ago (Acts 3:19-21)."

God is the God of restoration, making all things new again. He restores our souls (Psalm 23) and gives us new life. Throughout the gospels, (Matthew 9:2-8; Mark 7: 31-37; Mark 8:22-26; Luke 5:12-

25), we see the evidence of God's restorative powers in the lives of those Jesus touched. What Jesus did then, He continues to do now. He is the same yesterday, today and tomorrow (Hebrews 13:8) and will never leave us. The work Jesus was sent to do on the Cross works within us today. His blood covers our sin and brings us to repentance before God. No matter our particular brand of sin, it is not so big that Christ can't or won't forgive when we ask.

"For thus says the One who is high and lifted up, who inhabits eternity, whose name is Holy: 'I dwell in the high and holy place, and also with him who is of a contrite and lowly spirit, to revive the spirit of the lowly, and to revive the heart of the contrite' (Isaiah 57:15)."

Delight Yourself

"Trust in the Lord and do good; dwell in the land and befriend faithfulness. Delight yourself in the Lord, and He will give you the desires of your heart."
~Psalm 37:3-4

I've heard many Christians repeat this verse, especially verse 4, as if it's the magic key to Heaven. I've heard preachers give sermons on delighting in the Lord that sounded like a discourse on why they prospered, and the congregation didn't. I'm not saying there is anything wrong with material gain or having money. I like having money because I like boots and money allows me to have new boots...lots of them! I like being able to get from week to week without wondering how to pay the light bill or worrying about being able to keep my dogs' Barkbox™ bill paid. In the long run, boots and Barkbox™ are things I don't need but they certainly fall into the category of "desires." However, in the biblical context, delighting in the Lord and the desires of our hearts has a different meaning that has nothing to do with material wealth, wants, or needs.

God isn't about the wealth of this world, and why should He be? *It all belongs to Him anyway!* What He is concerned about is the state of our hearts and minds. When we pursue wealth and material desires, our minds become focused on that, which can lead to a dogged pursuit of something we never have enough of and will go to any lengths, even illegal ones, to possess. How many people get into trouble over money? How many people commit robbery and murder to have the things they want? The pursuit of getting what we don't have knows no class, race, age, or social standing and in the end, it's simply selfishness and greed that motivates people to get what they want at any cost. And that takes us far away from delighting in the Lord.

"The Lord is near to all who call on Him, to all who call on Him in truth. He fulfills the desire of those who fear Him; He also hears their cry and saves them. (Psalm 145:18-19)."

God's ways and our ways are often two very different things—God acts out of generosity and love, while we act out of selfish desires. But delighting in the Lord is the first step to aligning our will with His. Delighting in the Lord is wanting what He wants, saying what He says, doing what He does. It is coming to a place where our worth is found in Him and not in the things of this world. Some of the greatest figures in the Bible, like Noah, Job, David and Paul, delighted themselves in the Lord. They took true joy in knowing God and following Him, but it didn't mean they had an easy life.

Noah and his family were the only people spared when God destroyed the Earth with the flood. Noah was a righteous man, but he spent roughly 100 years building the ark and getting the animals on board. Job was a wealthy man who delighted in the Lord, but he wasn't spared great loss or physical pain when the devil came calling. David was a shepherd boy with nothing who became a wealthy king with everything. He is described as a man after God's own heart but that didn't keep him from great loss, betrayal, and threats against his life. Paul persecuted Christians until he met Jesus on Damascus road. He spent the rest of his life serving the Lord, which often meant being homeless, hungry, shipwrecked or in jail. All these people delighted in the Lord and had the desires of their hearts, which was to know the Lord their God intimately and fully. When we delight in something, we desire that thing. We pursue that thing. We go to any lengths to have that thing. The same thing happens when we delight in the Lord.

"Whom have I in heaven but You? And there is nothing on Earth that I desire besides You. My flesh and my heart may fail, but God is the strength of my heart and my portion forever. For behold, those who are far from You shall perish; You put an end to everyone who is unfaithful to You. But for me it is good to be near God; I have made the Lord God my refuge, that I may tell of all Your works (Psalm 73:25-28)."

To Immerse or Not

"Let all the house of Israel therefore know for certain that God has made Him both Lord and Christ, this Jesus whom you crucified." Now when they heard this they were cut to the heart and said to Peter and the rest of the apostles, "Brothers, what shall we do?" And Peter said to them, "Repent and be baptized every one of you in the name of Jesus Christ for the forgiveness of your sins, and you will receive the gift of the Holy Spirit. For the promise is for you and for your children and for all who are far off, everyone whom the Lord our God calls to Himself." And with many other words he bore witness and continued to exhort them, saying, "Save yourselves from this crooked generation." So those who received his word were baptized, and there were added that day about three thousand souls."
~Acts 2:36-41

My husband, Nathan's last birthday was a special day—I had the privilege of baptizing him. He took a long time to come to the Lord but when he did, he wanted to be baptized in the river. As this day has drawn closer, I've been thinking more and more about what to say during the baptism. I know to most, it seems like a simple event but for me, this is special. It's like marriage—sacred, and like marriage, a covenant between the person being baptized and the Lord.

I have been baptized three times. The first time, I was 18 and had accepted Christ as my Lord and Savior; the second time was when my late husband, Bear and two of our kids were baptized. I felt as if being baptized as a family was important for all of us. We were baptized by full immersion in water, in the Name of the Father, Son & Holy Spirit. Some years later, I began attending a church that believes being baptized in any way except the Name of Jesus, is incorrect, and I was baptized for the third time.

I have thought about this a lot, probably too much because that's me, but I am not convinced I would go to hell for failure to be baptized in the Name of Jesus only. On the other hand, I complied because the pastor was so adamant about this belief and what did it hurt for me to get wet again?

"The times of ignorance God overlooked, but now He commands all people everywhere to repent, be-cause He has fixed a day on which He will judge the world in righteousness by a Man whom He has ap-pointed; and of this He has given assurance to all by raising Him from the dead (Acts 17:30-31)."

There is no doubt salvation comes through re-pentance. Without repentance, baptism is just a bath and does nothing for the person being dunked. So, baptism is the second step in salvation—first, we accept Christ as our Savior by confessing our sins for forgiveness, and second, we are baptized by immer-sion. This helps us to identify with Christ's resurrec-tion. We go under the water, burying our old selves, and come up out of the water, resurrected into a brand-new life. I find nowhere in the Bible where anyone was sprinkled with water, and I find nowhere that infants were baptized. In order to repent, one must be old enough to understand sin, therefore, baptizing anyone unable to understand what they are doing has no point.

Jesus was baptized by John the Baptist, who had been baptizing people for some time by full immersion in the Jordan River. When Jesus came along, John baptized Him as well. When Jesus came up out of the water, the heavens opened, and God spoke. (Matthew 3:13-17). Now, there is no record of what John said when he baptized people, but I imagine it was in the Name of the Father.

"Now the eleven disciples went to Galilee, to the mountain to which Jesus had directed them. And when they saw Him they worshiped Him, but some doubted. And Jesus came and said to them, 'All authority in Heaven and on Earth has been given to Me. Go therefore and make disciples of all nations, baptizing them in the Name of the Father and of the Son and of the Holy Spirit, teaching them to observe all that I have commanded you. And behold, I am with you always, to the end of the age' (Matthew 28:16-20)."

Clearly, Jesus says to baptize in the Name of the Father, Son and Holy Spirit, so why was I told I had to be baptized again in the Name of Jesus for my baptism to count? The reason is in Acts Chapter Two. Jesus had been crucified, buried, and rose again. He had spent forty days on Earth with His disciples and they watched Him ascend into Heaven. What we don't know is everything Jesus taught during those forty days but Acts 2 was written about what the disciples did immediately following Christ's ascension. (Acts 1 retells of Christ's ascension and replacing Judas Iscariot). This is the account of Pentecost, when the Holy Spirit fell on everyone present and they spoke in other tongues and were endued with power from God. In verse 38, Peter tells the people to *"repent and be baptized in the Name of Jesus."*

Things had changed for the disciples. They were now the ones left to teach what Jesus taught, to lay hands on people, to heal the sick, and raise the dead. The disciples had felt the power of God descend on them through the Holy Spirit, the same thing that happened to Jesus immediately following His baptism.

Do I think if someone has been baptized in the Name of the Father, Son and Holy Spirit and dies, that they will go to hell? No. I do think that if a person was baptized as an infant or did not understand what or why, they do need to be instructed and baptized again, but only after repentance. If someone was baptized by sprinkling or pouring of water, I think they do need to be baptized by full immersion. Our sole reason for baptism is to identify with the burial and resurrection of Jesus Christ, and full immersion is the way to do that.

Baptism also infills us with the Holy Spirit, so when Peter, who spent so much time with Christ says, *"Be baptized in the Name of Jesus,"* and we have the chance to do so, we should be re-baptized. Or if it's our first baptism, we should make sure our pastor, or whoever is doing the baptizing, understands we want to be baptized in Jesus' Name.

"Brothers, I may say to you with confidence about the patriarch David that he both died and was buried, and his tomb is with us to this day. Being therefore a prophet and knowing that God had sworn with an oath to him that he would set one of his descendants on his throne, he foresaw and spoke about

the resurrection of the Christ, that He was not abandoned to Hades, nor did His flesh see corrupttion. This Jesus God raised up, and of that, we all are witnesses. Being therefore exalted at the right hand of God and having received from the Father the promise of the Holy Spirit, He has poured out this that you yourselves are seeing and hearing (Acts 2:29-33)."

A Smidgeon of Faith

"Though you have not seen Him, you love Him. Though you do not now see Him, you believe in Him and rejoice with joy that is inexpressible and filled with glory, obtaining the outcome of your faith, the salvation of your souls."
~1 Peter 1:8-9

I remember when I was a little girl my cousins and I played with dolls. We spoke for them, made up places they went, events that happened, and married Barbie and Ken over and over again. It was called 'make believe' and as a parent, I listened as my kids played games of make believe. A chair and pillow became a car, a cardboard box was a treasure chest spilling gold and jewels onto the ground, and my kids were teachers, doctors, cowboys, and Indians. Make believe is great fun. It's when we get older that we realize make believe is for kids and we must face the reality of being a responsible adult.

But what happens when we are told Jesus is make believe? We pray to a God we can't see; we wait for miracles from a Lord that isn't visible; and we hope for salvation that will be fulfilled when He returns, or we die and go to a place called Heaven. How do we reconcile ourselves to believing in what many call 'make believe' when it comes to the Bible?

"At that time the disciples came to Jesus, saying, 'Who is the greatest in the kingdom of Heaven?' And calling to Him a child, He put him in the midst of them and said, 'Truly, I say to you, unless you turn and become like children, you will never enter the

kingdom of Heaven. Whoever humbles himself like this child is the greatest in the kingdom of Heaven' (Matthew 18:1-4)."

Children are so trusting and have no hang ups about being honest and open. I remember when my son, Michael, was being potty trained. My late husband was in prison, so the only man around was my next-door neighbor. I asked him to help me, so he took my son out back and showed him how to pee on a tree. Michael was tree trained from that day forward. One day, we were walking downtown and there were trees planted every so often at the edge of the sidewalk, and I noticed Michael was no longer beside me. I turned around and there's my son with his pants at his knees, watering the tree. Of course, he was three at the time and passersby chuckled. My son had no shame, no fear of reprisal, and he wasn't embarrassed. That's how we believe in Jesus—without shame or embarrassment, no matter what anyone else might say.

"That the God of our Lord Jesus Christ, the Father of glory, may give you the Spirit of wisdom and of revelation in the knowledge of Him, having the eyes of your hearts enlightened, that you may know what is the hope to which He has called you, what are the riches of His glorious inheritance in the saints (Ephesians 1:17-18)."

I have been mocked and ridiculed for my faith. Once or twice it hurt my feelings but in the long run, those are the people I pray for the most. I know their minds have been blinded to the truth of Jesus Christ. It takes just a smidgeon of faith to be saved by confessing Christ is Lord, and I pray for everyone to have just that much faith because I know if they take that first shaky step, the Holy Spirit will multiply that faith more and more with each successive step. And with faith comes hope, peace and joy in what we cannot see with our eyes but with our spirit.

"In Him we have redemption through His blood, the forgiveness of our trespasses, according to the riches of His grace, which He lavished upon us, in all wisdom and insight making known to us the mystery of His will, according to His purpose, which He set forth in Christ as a plan for the fullness of time, to unite all things in Him, things in Heaven and things on Earth (Ephesians 1:7-10)."

A Few Gray Hairs

"So we do not lose heart. Though our outer self is wasting away, our inner self is being renewed day by day. For this light momentary affliction is pre-paring for us an eternal weight of glory beyond all comparison, as we look not to the things that are seen but to the things that are unseen. For the things that are seen are transient, but the things that are unseen are eternal."
~ 2 Corinthians 4:16-18

I had laser surgery for secondary cataracts. This is a condition that has a low occurrence after cataract surgery when new lenses are implanted, which I had in 2015. The actual laser procedure takes less than a minute and is completely painless. The results are amazing, except for the floaters I had that settle down within a few days. The biggest difference was how much better my vision in my left eye was than my right, which I always referred to as my "good eye." However, the secondary cataract in the right eye wasn't big enough for the laser to work, so I have to wait until it is.

"Even to your old age I will be the same, and even to your graying years I will bear you! I have done it, and I will carry you; and I will bear you and I will deliver you. (Isaiah 46:4)."

We call it aging. Our hair turns silver, or in my case, snow white, lines appear on our faces, skin sags, our energy levels decrease, we have aches and pains, arthritis sets in, our hearing isn't as good, and our vision begins to go. I always say old age isn't for sissies! Everything around us seems to be geared toward the younger generations. Clothing, activities, music, movies etc. and while youth may be wasted on the young, it's good to know that God loves us old folks too.

"But ask the beasts, and they will teach you; the birds of the heavens, and they will tell you; or the bushes of the Earth, and they will teach you; and the fish of the sea will declare to you. Who among all these does not know that the hand of the Lord has done this? In His hand is the life of every living thing and the breath of all mankind. Does not the ear test words as the palate tastes food? Wisdom is with the aged and understanding in length of days (Job 12:7-12)."

There is something very comforting to me about being older; having the insanity of my youth behind me, and a wisdom that comes only from living life and learning from it. Being young is full of stress, worry, strife, difficulties, and each step forward seems fraught with an undiscernible future. Trying to reel life in isn't easy, and none of us were born with an instruction booklet. It can feel as if we are just left to flounder on our own and hope it turns out all right. But growing older in life and growing up in the Lord at the same time is a wonderful place to be. Learning to live in your own skin, coming to grips with your regrets, and settling into who you are instead of all the compartmentalized aspects of life is very comforting. Despite the physical degeneration, life has never looked better.

"The righteous flourish like the palm tree and grow like a cedar in Lebanon. They are planted in the house of the Lord; they flourish in the courts of our

God. They still bear fruit in old age; they are ever full of sap and green, to declare that the Lord is upright; He is my rock, and there is no unrighteousness in Him (Psalm 92:12-15)."

Whisper Hope

*"When his vision came round there was a young girl
on the ground
And he knew she was finding it hard to cope
She never was a fighter until he laid beside her
And gently whispered hope
They got up to their feet and they sang Hallelujah
People in the street were turning around
They looked them in the eyes and they sang Hallelu-
jah
Oh, there's someone here that we have found
They sang, Hallelujah, Hallelujah
We are the voices crying in the wilderness
Hallelujah, Hallelujah
The people in the street started their sins to confess
and a chorus of
Hallelujah, Hallelujah
Hallelujah, Hallelujah
Every knee will bow, and every tongue confess
And the voice of one crying in the wilderness
Crying out Hallelujah, Hallelujah."
~Lyrics from Gabriel and the Vagabond by Foy Vance*

This is from one of my favorite songs by Foy Vance on his album, *Hope*. It doesn't take much to give someone the hope that tomorrow is going to be a better day, or that their life is worth living. For some, life seems to be a series of disasters lined up like thunder clouds in the distance. For others, life seems to come up roses no matter what they do. The disparity between us can sometimes feel unfair and not worth the trouble. But when we look at others to compare ourselves, we are always going to come up lacking. That is part of the problem in our world to-

day; we are so commercialized and constantly inun-
dated with the idea that if we have more, bigger,
better, shinier, and newer things, our lives will be
better, happier, and successful. In reality, it's a lie
being sold by an industry that is not in the least bit
concerned about anyone's happiness or success, they
are interested in lining their pockets with our
money.

There's a line from a movie where the actor
plays a person who makes commercials: "It's sell,
sell, sell and we're all going to hell, but here's a big,
fat check to smooth out the ride." Yet, in the midst
of all our wealth and the mountains of things that
we own, the number of people who are in therapy
and on drugs for depression and anxiety are at an
all-time high. There is something very wrong with
our priorities and how we live our lives.

*"Rejoice in the Lord always; again I will say, re-
joice. Let your reasonableness be known to everyone. The Lord is at hand; do not be anxious about
anything, but in everything by prayer and supplica-
tion with thanksgiving let your requests be made
known to God. And the peace of God, which surpasses all understanding, will guard your hearts and
your minds in Christ Jesus. Finally, brothers, whatever is true, whatever is honorable, whatever is
just, whatever is pure, whatever is lovely, whatever
is commendable, if there is any excellence, if there
is anything worthy of praise, think about these
things. What you have learned and received and
heard and seen in me—practice these things, and the
God of peace will be with you (Philippians 4:4-10)."*

I like putting the first words in verse 4 with

the last words of verse 10: *Rejoice in the Lord and the God of peace will be with you.* What we need for peace and happiness will never come from what we can buy, it will always come from what we find inside of us through a relationship with Jesus Christ. That's not to say we won't have trials. Our children won't suddenly become angels, and our spouses won't become some 50's TV show idea of marriage, and the bills will still show up on a regular basis, but when we have the peace of Christ within us, those things won't be our focus. And what we focus on is what we pursue.

"But those who desire to be rich fall into temptation, into a snare, into many senseless and harmful desires that plunge people into ruin and destruction. For the love of money is a root of all kinds of evils. It is through this craving that some have wandered away from the faith and pierced themselves with many pangs. But as for you, O man of God, flee these things. Pursue righteousness, godliness, faith, love, steadfastness, gentleness. Fight the good fight of the faith. Take hold of the eternal life to which you were called and about which you made the good confession in the presence of many witnesses (1 Timothy 6:9-12)."

When we pursue righteousness, godliness, faith, love, steadfastness, and gentleness, fighting the good fight of faith, we are also called to help others. Hopelessness is all around us, but it doesn't take much to share our hope and faith with those in need. Hope can be seen just as hopelessness can be seen, and it takes so little to share real hope with another person. We are the hope of Jesus Christ to someone who has no hope for tomorrow, so share!

"Blessed be the God and Father of our Lord Jesus Christ! According to His great mercy, He has caused us to be born again to a living hope through the resurrection of Jesus Christ from the dead, to an inheritance that is imperishable, undefiled, and unfading, kept in Heaven for you, who by God's power are being guarded through faith for a salvation ready to be revealed in the last time. In this you rejoice, though now for a little while, if necessary, you have been grieved by various trials, so that the tested genuineness of your faith—more precious than gold that perishes though it is tested by fire—may be found to result in praise and glory and honor at the revelation of Jesus Christ (1 Peter 1:3-7)."

Something To Believe In

"That the God of our Lord Jesus Christ, the Father of glory, may give you the Spirit of wisdom and of revelation in the knowledge of Him, having the eyes of your hearts enlightened, that you may know what is the hope to which He has called you, what are the riches of His glorious inheritance in the saints, and what is the immeasurable greatness of His power toward us who believe, according to the working of His great might that He worked in Christ when He raised Him from the dead and seated Him at His right hand in the heavenly places."
~ Ephesians 1:17-20

When we are children, our world is confined to the house we live in, our parents, siblings, and perhaps, grandparents or other extended family members. And we are perfectly content in that world. As we grow, our world expands to include school, friends, and outside activities. Our world continues to grow larger the older we get. There eventually comes a point when we want to know what is beyond our city, state, and even our country.

It's a big world and we often feel the need to explore whatever it is we think lies outside of our view. It's how the world was conquered. If not for those who wanted to know what lay beyond the great oceans, the New World would not have been discovered. If there had never been anyone who looked into the sky and thought, *what if I could build a rocket to take someone there*, Neil Armstrong would have never set foot on the moon. We have an inborn desire to know who we are, where we came from, and why we are here. People have traveled millions of miles, built monuments to un-known gods, and traversed the stars seeking answers only to find they still have questions. We are all simply searching for something bigger than ourselves to believe in.

"By faith we understand that the universe was cre-ated by the word of God, so that what is seen was not made out of things that are visible (Hebrews 11:3)."

Belief in anything takes faith. If you go rock climbing, you have faith in your gear and your train-ing so that you don't plummet to your death. When you jump out of an airplane at 13,000 feet, you have faith that when you pull the cord, the parachute will open. Every morning when you jump into your car to go to work, you have faith that turning the key will start the engine. Everything we do requires some be-lief that what we are doing will succeed.

But what about the biggest questions of all – is there a God? If there is a God, why is planet Earth so messed up? What is the purpose of life in the grand scheme of things? Why am I here? Those are ques-tions I've had too. And after a lot of exploration and faith in things that did not matter, or were not good for me, I concluded that no amount of education or knowledge of this world is going to answer those questions for me. Those answers were inside of me my whole life and are completely answered by faith and belief.

"And without faith it is impossible to please Him, for whoever would draw near to God must believe that He exists and that He rewards those who seek

Him (Hebrews 11:6)."

We are born with a God-shaped hole inside of us. I tried to fill mine with everything but God, and I was never satisfied until I filled it with the Word of God. No, I didn't conclude that Jesus was the answer because there was suddenly some enlightened place inside of me; I concluded Jesus was the answer because all else had failed. Nothing I had tried in life fulfilled me, nothing had made me feel as if I had the answers, and almost everyone in my life had let me down. Yet I knew somewhere deep down inside there had to be an answer, there had to be more, and when I was out of answers, God gave me His.

"There is salvation in no one else, for there is no other name under Heaven given among men by which we must be saved (Acts 4:12)."

God created everything that is created from nothing. He spoke it into existence. He also gave us that desire to create, to explore, to expand, to reach for more. But He never intended for us to do it without Him. That is where people went wrong. We became more, had more, did more, went farther and created monuments, not to unknown gods, but to ourselves. We stepped outside the scope of creation in the false belief that we could do it ourselves. That's why, no matter how successful we are or what we accomplish, we still feel unfulfilled. That God-shaped hole can only be filled by one person—Jesus Christ.

"Since then we have a great high priest who has passed through the heavens, Jesus, the Son of

God, let us hold fast our confession. For we do not have a High Priest who is unable to sympathize with our weaknesses, but one who in every respect has been tempted as we are, yet without sin. Let us then with confidence draw near to the throne of grace, that we may receive mercy and find grace to help in time of need (Hebrews 4:14-16)."

The Path of Righteousness

"The Lord is my Shepherd; I shall not want. He makes me lie down in green pastures. He leads me beside still waters. He restores my soul. He leads me in paths of righteousness for His name's sake. Even though I walk through the valley of the shadow of death, I will fear no evil, for You are with me; Your rod and your staff, they comfort me. You prepare a table before me in the presence of my enemies, You anoint my head with oil; my cup overflows. Surely goodness and mercy shall follow me all the days of my life, and I shall dwell in the house of the Lord forever."
~Psalm 23

Some of the most touching and powerful prayers are in the book of Psalms. In King David's psalms, there is much heartache, heartbreak, fear, and loneliness, but there is also much joy. David knew God was with him no matter the circumstance. He experienced great highs and great lows but his faith that God would deliver him never wavered. We, like David, also experience these same times of great highs and great lows, but are we always sure God is with us? The strength of our faith will determine how we handle the ups and downs of life.

Verse 1: *The Lord is my Shepherd; I shall not want.* A shepherd is one who keeps the sheep from danger. He will go to any lengths to fight off wild animals to keep his sheep safe. If we truly believe the Lord is our Shepherd, how much further will He go to keep us safe? The shepherd makes sure his sheep are fed and watered, they have no need to go in search of

110

food because the shepherd provides for them. They want for nothing, and when we depend upon the Lord, neither will we (Philippians 4:19-20).

Verse 2: *He leads me beside still waters.*
Sheep can't drink from running waters, it has to do with the shape of their mouths. They must have a still pool to drink from to satisfy their thirst. Still waters also indicate peace, so when we trust the Lord, He will make sure we have His peace, no matter what's going on in our lives (Ephesians 2:19).

Verse 3: *He restores my soul. He leads me in paths of righteousness for His name's sake.*
When we live in sin, our souls are in turmoil but when we have our lives in Christ, our souls are at peace. They have been completely restored by Jesus. He becomes our Shepherd and directs our paths for His name's sake. Why? So that He will be glorified. We are the glory of God and when we walk the path He has for us, everything we do will glorify Him to the rest of the world (2 Corinthians 13:5).

Verse 4: *Even though I walk through the valley of the shadow of death, I will fear no evil, for You are with me; Your rod and Your staff, they comfort me.*
The valleys we walk through can be dark and fearsome. The events in life can make us feel like life isn't worth living, or if a lot of traumatic events have taken place in our lives, we can live in constant fear that something else is going to happen. But when we walk the paths of righteousness in Christ Jesus, we do not have to fear because He is our comfort (2 Corinthians 1:3-4). When we trust com-

pletely in Him, our fears are put to rest.

Verse 5: *You prepare a table before me in the presence of my enemies; You anoint my head with oil; my cup overflows.*
I love this verse. Imagine your enemies all around you, the way they were David, yet, in the midst of chaos, you sit down to eat the finest meal you've ever imagined, without a care in the world. I think it would blow the enemies' minds! Jesus is like that.

      He will lead us right through the fire without letting us get singed even a little bit. He anoints us with heavenly oil that marks us as belonging to the only true King, Him! He provides for us to the point that no matter what we do, we can't contain the provision that is pressed down, shaken together and running over (Luke 6:38). Our Shepherd cares for us, keeps us, loves us, provides for us beyond anything we can ever imagine.

Verse 6: *Surely goodness and mercy shall follow me all the days of my life, and I shall dwell in the house of the Lord forever.*
Because of Christ's immense love for us, He pours out His goodness and mercy upon us all the days of our lives. We are His children, and like any proud daddy, He wants to give us everything we need. Of course, we will have trials in life but that's just how a fallen world works, but unlike those who drudge through, we, the children of the Most High, can walk through life with our shoulders back and our heads held high. If God is for us, who can be against us (Romans 8:31)? We have all that Heaven offers through the blood of Jesus Christ and in the end, we will realize the fullness of that love when we step

from this life into everlasting life in Heaven. We will dwell in the Lord's house forever.

No matter what is going on in your life, Jesus Christ is with you and He will not leave you (Deuteronomy 31:8). Your Shepherd is with you and He will protect you.

Other books by Marie McGaha also available from DWB
www.dwbpublishing.com

When God Talks, It's Time To Listen

Comfort & Joy book one: forgiveness

The Root, The Shoot, The Fruit

Shine His Light Lessons In Life

Visit Marie's website for all her books, including her line of romantic fiction

www.mariemcgaha.com

www.ingramcontent.com/pod-product-compliance
Lightning Source LLC
Chambersburg PA
CBHW020551030426
42337CB00013B/1054